Perfect
Strangers
A Memoir of the Swinging 70's

Dorothy's works appear in numerous anthologies including:

Best Women's Erotica Of The Year Vol.1

For The Men And The Women Who Love Them

The Sexy Librarian's Dirty 30, Vol. 2

Dirty Old Women, Dirty 30 Anthology Vol.2

The Big Book Of Submission Vol.2

Tonight, She's Yours: Cuckold Fantasies II

And now, *Perfect Strangers*

Perfect Strangers

A Memoir of the Swinging 70's

BY
DOROTHY FREED

Advance Praise for *Perfect Strangers*

"Dorothy Freed walks readers through the swinging 70's, showing the very personal impact of the sexual revolution on her life as she goes from wife to erotic explorer."

> —**Rachel Kramer Bussel**
> **Editor of *BEST WOMEN'S EROTICA OF THE YEAR, VOL's, 1-3* and over 60 other erotica anthologies.**

"PERFECT STRANGERS: A Memoir of the Swinging Seventies, a decidedly sex-positive memoir, takes the reader along for the ride as newly divorced Dorothy Freed undertakes an erotic journey into the real contours of the sexual revolution, seeking to discover her pathway to orgasm. Her story demonstrates just how hot the process of writing oneself whole can be!"

> —**Jen Cross**
> **Founder/facilitator and author of *Writing Ourselves Whole*, co-editor of *Sex Still Spoken Here*, and co-facilitator of the Erotic Reading Circle.**

To my amazing second husband, Lee.
A man well worth waiting for.

Table Of Contents

Foreword
Carol Queen, Ph.D. 1

Part One – 1974
Whatever Happened To Happily Ever After?
Chapter One 7

Part Two – 1975
Will You Marry Me?
Chapter Two 23

Perfect Stranger Encounter #1, James 36
Chapter Three 44

Part Three – 1976
Libra And Pisces And Cancer, Oh My!
Chapter Four 56

Perfect Stranger Encounter #2, Steve 64
Chapter Five 72

Perfect Stranger Encounter #3, Light Angel 78

Perfect Stranger Encounter #4, Jake 88
Chapter Six 106

Perfect Stranger Encounter #5, Three-Way 120

Perfect Stranger Encounter #6, The Foursome 128

Part Four – 1976-1977
A Gaggle Of Geese, A Stable Of Studs 138
Chapter Seven 144

Perfect Stranger Encounter #7, The Gambler 156

Perfect Stranger Encounter #8, Alan 164
      Chapter Eight 172
      Chapter Nine 186
      Chapter Ten 192

Perfect Stranger Encounter #9, Stuart 196
      Chapter Eleven 204

Perfect Stranger Encounter #10, Paul 208
      Chapter Twelve 217

Part Five – 1977
How Many Notches Do I Make On My Gun,
Before The Handle Falls Off? 223
      Chapter Thirteen 227

Perfect Stranger Encounter #11, Jake
And A Green-Eyed Stranger 233
      Chapter Fourteen 245

Epilogue
The Other Side, Of The Other Side,
Of The Rainbow 253

About Dorothy Freed 260

More Stories by Dorothy Freed 261

Foreword

Carol Queen Ph.D.

One of the reasons I've been devoted to the Erotic Reading Circle for most of the last 25 years—first at Good Vibrations, where it began, and then at the Center for Sex and Culture, in San Francisco, where it's held now—is repeatedly experiencing the thrill of hearing a fantastic new story or a strong new voice. People come to the Circle as established writers or as absolute beginners, seeking feedback for the last edit before publication or bringing old journal entries or a first-time story into the light. It's diverse in so many ways, full of surprises, light-bulb moments and unexpected pleasures. And I experienced this the initial night we were visited by Dorothy Freed, sharing the first episode of her creative non-fiction memoir with us. I'm so happy that now it's ready to share with you.

I urged Dorothy to keep writing for many reasons, but perhaps the first was the way her very real, expressive story opens a door in time, taking the listener or reader back to another reality: San Francisco in the 1970s. After the Summer of Love had its way with the city, San Francisco opened its arms to more and more seekers of every kind of enlightenment, including sexual. We've heard a lot about gay men in that decade flooding to the most open city in our country for their loves and lusts—but we don't hear as much about women, raised to be heterosexual Doris Day clones, but touched and changed by feminism, dreams of woman's empowerment and alternative life paths. That's the story Dorothy tells, the life that a wide-open decade in this wide-open town made possible. It's complicated and full of the details that made me, too, fall in love with San Francisco when I first came to the City by the Bay. Many people have left their hearts in San Francisco—but Dorothy didn't do that because she stayed.

Maybe some people's love affair with San Francisco comes without the added bonus of love affairs with its people, but those affairs are Dorothy's Pilgrim Progress as she addresses issues that will resonate with many of her readers, especially women. She starts out afflicted with what Betty Friedan, in her 1963 best-selling book The Feminine Mystique called "the problem that has no name," the anomie of a woman trying to live in a sexist and suppressing marriage. She feels minimized, to the point of faking vaginal orgasms to gain her husband's approval, and feels sexually inferior to her husband's lover, a woman capable of vaginal orgasm—and who takes off with Dorothy's husband.

We don't usually read "the problem that has no name" as sexual frustration. But Dorothy's story illustrates the need for a sexual revolution specific to women's situations: the way women were trapped in their expected roles just started with the gendered jobs of childcare and housework, then very much extended to sexuality. Dorothy is baffled at her husband's accusation that she's "frigid"—pretty much a synonym for "not vaginally orgasmic," or as the feminists of that era preferred to call it, pre-orgasmic. A post-war woman lucky enough to "have it all"—a husband, perfect kids, a house in the suburbs, possibly even a college degree and a job of her own—could feel like less than a real woman if she wasn't sexually responsive, no matter what her husband did or didn't know about pleasing her. And lest you think of this as a stone-age story from an era before we all got enlightened, remember that many women today still have no idea that perhaps only about 25 percent of women orgasm from intercourse alone. Penile thrusting wasn't sufficient for the majority of women in the 1960s, and it's not enough now...which makes Dorothy's explorations and discoveries far more than historical fiction or reminiscence.

So, starting out like many other women whose own sexual revolution in the 1960s required seizing their self-esteem and shaking off outdated expectations, the way Dorothy saves herself once she splits for San Francisco has everything to do with independence and erotic exploration (or, as she prefers to call it, "rampant promiscuity"). Man after man (oh, and a woman or two!) enters her life, each one a journey in and out of the sheets, each one adding to Dorothy's gradually growing understanding of what she really wants and needs in her life.

I've said it countless times: Sex education is so terrible in the United States that for many people, promiscuity is the most accessible way to learn about sex and what they want from it. Some elements of this oft-reviled yet commonly practiced lifestyle are in fact positive and freeing, then and now. Dorothy sets out to learn not just about pleasure, but about people—and most importantly, how she wants to experience both. Since we are living now in the age of Tindr and other so-called "dating" apps—although clearly some people cut right to the chase—it's worth pointing out that there are young women right this minute on a quest of the kind Dorothy undertook forty-plus years ago. Sure, they can call up partners and sexual scenarios on their smartphones rather than seeking out an alternative newspaper with its classified ads. But erotic empowerment is easier to find with a solid knowledge base, and today's isn't always much better than Dorothy's was decades ago when she began her quest.

Along the way, we are treated to images of life in a decade that's both hidden in the past and simultaneously underlies our own historical moment like a wavy mirror image. All the many changes in sex, racial and sexual identity politics, family structure, gendered power dynamics, and more will seem at least

4

a little familiar. Reading Dorothy's story from one perspective lets us see the skeletons of all the movements that have become part of our lives since the late 20th century; we see early snapshots of cultural changes we've been living out ever since. We don't just see some of the roots of feminism and sex-positivity; we also get a view of a time before AIDS (but not VD), before Black Lives Matter (but not the Black Panthers and highly-felt emotion about race).

Today we live in a world full of relationship explorers, polyamorists, and open relationship enthusiasts—in addition to some players and cheaters, who certainly haven't left the scene. Some of Dorothy's lovers and Dorothy herself helped our community grow to accommodate open marriage, easy sex with fuck buddies, and other attempts to wed connection and freedom. The sexual and identity-politics culture of the 1960s and 70s are very much the predecessors of all of these movements that seem so contemporary: feminism, LGBT rights, blended families and single parents, and the search for intimacy and self-esteem.

Readers may or may not relate to the way Dorothy lives, but these chapters, sexy as they can be, aren't just erotica. (Not that there's anything at all wrong with "just" a sexy narrative!) Unlike so many other stories, sex isn't alluded to—it's lived and co-experienced as you turn each page. And I hope readers will see all the other elements of Dorothy's life that her sexy times are inextricably linked to what it means to be a divorced mom responsibly raising sons; the link and (sometimes) the disconnect between emotional relating and erotic experience; and the way that having sex with someone helps you learn things about them, and about yourself.

Dorothy is over the rainbow in San Francisco: home of orgies, party houses and peep shows, the co-ed, sex-on-premises Sutro Bath House, the erotic glitz of the clubs on Broadway and Carol Doda's gigantic silicone breasts, and a community of diverse sexual seekers. With every adventure into pleasure, she is coming home to herself. And of course, that's not just a 70s experience. I wish that for your own adventures too, dear readers. Ride along as Dorothy learns the ropes of her own pleasures, then go do your own thing.

Carol Queen PhD
Founding Director, Center for Sex & Culture
San Francisco

Part One—1974

Whatever Happened to Happily Ever After?

CHAPTER ONE

When I discovered my husband, Paul, naked and on top of my best friend, Cassandra, it wasn't the infidelity that hurt me the most—it was the *sizzling sex* they were engaged in that cut to my core and changed my life forever. That's when my journey began.

The blinds were drawn so no one outside could see in, but from where I stood in the hallway at the entrance to Cassandra's bedroom, I could see them clearly enough in the light from a bedside lamp. They were naked. Paul was on top, hips pumping, leaning on his elbows. Cassandra's legs were wrapped tightly around his slim waist, hips rising to meet him as he plunged into her.

"You're so damned hot," he whispered, kissing her. "Come for me baby."

Obligingly, Cassandra's small moans of pleasure rose to a scream. Her large round ass raised right off the bed, her body stiffened, her toes curled, and her eyes rolled back in her head. She climaxed for what seemed like hours, while Paul gazed down at her in delight.

Twelve years of marriage, I thought bitterly. *We were never that hot!*

I was stunned by the sight of them, unable to move or even breathe. My loud, thumping heart flew around in my chest like a bird trapped in a chimney until I feared I might pass out. Glancing up, I saw myself dimly reflected in the wall mirror—a petite, dark-haired observer standing stiff with shock, watching the happy couple on the bed below. Pure rage welled up in me then, and I grabbed up a good-sized potted plant from Cassandra's mahogany desk near the doorway and hurled it as far as I could. It landed with a loud thud on the thickly carpeted floor a foot from the bed, spraying broken greenery, pottery shards, and bits of earth all over the room.

Paul, visibly shaken, leaped from the bed and pulled on his pants, his mouth a thin judgmental line. "Try to behave like an adult!" he snapped, attempting to take charge of the situation. But I was past any semblance of adult behavior at that point and began to scream and sob and berate them. Paul didn't appear to know what to do, and we might have gone on that way forever if Cassandra hadn't leaped out of bed like the cavalry arriving to avenge a massacre.

"You're so damned selfish, Dorothy!" she shrieked, taking my husband's hand. "Paul and I are in love, and you're standing in the way of our happiness. Look, we're compatible. You and Paul are not! Accept it. You have no Aquarius in your chart! I do! It's as simple as that!"

I don't know how simple it actually was, but the fight went out of me then, and I went into a quieter form of shock. Somehow I got home to bed, where I cocooned myself in blankets and cried for hours.

The beginning of the end of my marriage had come one bright May morning, when a new neighbor showed up at my door and introduced herself, offering friendship. I was hand-building a human figure from coils of clay in the corner of the garage that I referred to as my ceramic studio, when she arrived and introduced herself.

I looked up, reluctantly. I loved every moment of cutting into a wedge of moist clay and molding it into artwork. Studio time, which took place during the hours when my sons were in school, wedged, like the clay, between food shopping and household tasks, were precious to me. I went there to escape, think, and process life.

Cassandra came from LA and was more sophisticated than any of the women I knew in the suburbs of Syracuse New York. She was good looking in a tallish big-boned way with small high breasts and a large behind. She believed in astrology, tarot cards and all things New Age—and was the first woman I knew who openly discussed her husband's sexual performance, and claimed an ability to achieve vaginal orgasms.

That last bit of information impressed me mightily because I had difficulties having orgasms at all, and was hypersensitive about my lack of sexual response. Well, not lack, exactly. I did get excited during sex, very excited—especially during manual or oral sex—but not excited enough, and then it was over. Paul, who'd gone down on me briefly before penetration, fell asleep instantly, satisfied he'd done all he could to have pleased me—while I lay awake, high and dry, as the saying goes, agonizing over my inadequate response to lovemaking and consistent failure to orgasm with Paul inside me.

Cassandra caught me at a time when I was attempting to pinpoint why—in spite of two great kids, a house in the suburbs, and even an art degree from Syracuse University—everything a woman could want—I often felt frustrated and unfulfilled.

"A neighbor told me you're an artist," she said, smiling, eyeing my coil figure with interest. "I thought we might have something in common and here I am." Certainly, her outspoken conversation struck a more responsive chord in me than the local housewives I knew, who were deeply involved with Tide, chopped meat, and bowling.

10

Cassandra was an exciting new friend. She was my age, twenty-nine, and into ceramics, as I was, and lived in a big expensive house a few blocks from our modest neighborhood. It was so convenient for me to use her well-equipped pottery studio—and for her, as it turned out, to use my well-equipped husband while I experimented with stoneware sculpture. She had a husband of her own, but he spent most of his time away from home, working and mine appealed to her astrologically, and that was that. From the minute she met Paul and stared deeply into his eyes, the day of my divorce was imminent.

"It's no surprise you and Paul argue so much, Dorothy. I see many incompatibilities," she told me one morning over coffee and chart interpretation. She gave me a sympathetic look, then set her mug down on our Formica kitchen table and flipped through her copy of *How to Write Your Own Horoscope*.

"See, Paul has a water sign moon, and your chart lacks water," she commented, nodding her head for emphasis. "Now that's most likely the cause of your sexual problems—you do have sexual problems?" she inquired.

Surprised, I gawked at her, feeling my face flush with embarrassment, wondering how she could know that.

"I thought so," she said, tapping a page in the book, "Here's the reason. I'll explain it to you." And she went on an on with the astrology thing until I was hooked on it, too.

Astrology was in, in 1974, and so was I when I began discovering myself as a Virgo. I'd always been one, of course, but hadn't given it much thought before. Now, it became a thought-provoking study of the various aspects of my practical, order-loving, analytical personality and I saw myself in a whole new light. Cassandra assured me astrology could explain everything in my life. Well, maybe it could explain why being married since age seventeen to my *one-and-only* could turn out to be such a *big drag*. Maybe, astrology could tell me how Paul and I might, after all these years, become compatible.

I found the subject intriguing, but for Paul, astrology became a born-again kind of thing, introducing a new meaning to his life. Beginning with Cassandra's copy of Linda Goodman's, *Sun Signs,* he read everything available on the subject in general, and the nature of Aquarius in particular. "Key words he'd quote with satisfaction, "Humanitarian, unconventional, freedom-loving. Sounds like me, don't you think?"

"You've got a fascinating chart," Cassandra cooed in his ear one evening at our house, while her husband was working and our son's, Brad and Doug, were in bed. "Five planets in Aquarius—you'll be right at home in the Aquarian Age. I'll bet most people don't understand you, Paul. You're decades ahead of your time."

It wasn't easy living with Paul before this and

harder still once he became aware of his New Age Status.

Before astrology, our arguments, the keynote of our marriage, took the form of a parent/child lecture. Given our ten year age difference, Paul played the authoritarian parent; while I played the dissatisfied, demanding child. But thanks to Cassandra and the dawning of the Aquarian Age, we approached fighting in a new novel way.

"You think I'm insensitive?" Paul was outraged. "You've seen my chart? I'm idealistic and altruistic, which you'd appreciate if you weren't a detail-obsessed Virgo who can't see the forest for the trees!"

He intended to put me in my place, but I was studying astrology too. "Let's not forget your Cancer moon. You're crabby, cranky, moody, and emotionally insecure!"

Using his newfound knowledge, Paul compared me, unfavorably, to our friend Cassandra, whose primary astrological aspects were favorably aligned with his, making them highly compatible. "You're an uptight, perfectionistic Virgo," he snarled, "*and frigid in the bargain!*"

That shot hit home. Having read Sigmund Freud, I believed I had a frigidity problem because weren't women *supposed* to come with their husband's penis's inside them? But as long as I felt free to blame this on my mother and my middle-class upbringing, I felt somewhat let off the hook. Now, it seemed that I was born with the problem—*that my inability to achieve vaginal orgasm was written in the stars!* I gasped with hurt and struggled for a comeback, as Paul, narrow-eyed, informed me that my ability to be fully passionate was constricted by a Mars/Saturn square.

I am so passionate, you prick! I wanted to shout, but since Paul was my first and only lover, I had no counter opinion to offer. "And where on your chart does it indicate that you're overly controlling?" I inquired, instead.

"Listen, you unreasonable, shortsighted…" He turned bright red, stopped to catch his breath and attempted to be reasonable. "Dorothy, we're both feeling the influence of the Uranus transit through Libra. Uranus rules change; Libra rules partnerships. That's why our marriage is falling apart. Can't you even try to understand?"

"I understand. Take your Uranus transit and shove it!"

How times change. In the fifties, we repressed everything. In the sixties we expressed everything. Now here we were in in the mid-seventies, hurling planets. We threw signs, trines, conjunctions, and squares until our argument degenerated into "My sign's better than yours!

Even while Cassandra kindly opened my eyes to the unfavorable aspects of Paul's chart and mine, my eyes were still closed to what was happening between them. I don't know exactly when they began sleeping together, but small curls of suspicion began working their way into my mind over the next several months. For instance, I couldn't help noticing how much Paul enjoyed her company—and how he laughed and teased her and laid on the charm whenever she was around. Or the way she flattered his wit and intellect and smiled into his eyes.

Once, at a dinner party at Cassandra's, I caught a long, intimate look between them that chilled me. I brought it up to Paul, seeking reassurance, but he was outraged by what he called my insecure, suspicious nature, due to some planetary placement on my chart.

"We're three good friends who hang out together, *nothing more*," he declared, and feeling foolish, I believed Paul's words and apologized for my lack of trust. Frequent disagreements and lackluster sex life aside, we were, after all, happily married.

I believed that until the chilly February morning when I dropped in on Cassandra, intending to use her studio while the kids were in school and I *thought* Paul was working. I knew she was home because her car was in the driveway. But she wasn't in the studio, or the spacious kitchen with the new avocado green appliances, or the living room with the oriental carpets on the floor, and a hand-built ceramic vase on the polished oak coffee table. Thinking she might be napping, I walked silently down the wood-paneled hallway to her bedroom.

That's when I found them in bed together—and any lingering illusions about the success of my marriage were finally shot to hell.

By evening I pulled myself together enough to tell Brad, age eleven, and seven-year-old Doug, that I wasn't feeling well so we'd be visiting Grandma in New York City for a few weeks. "You'll have a good time," I said, forcing a smile. "She'll cook your favorite foods and take you to the movies." *And I need time to rest and think*

Paul returned home later, after the kids were asleep, joining me in our cramped bedroom with its mismatched furniture and worn old bedspread. The room was hot and stuffy. Outside, a heavy winter wind blew sheets of icy rain, steadily and annoyingly against the side of the house. I had a king-sized headache and lay on the bed with an ice pack on my forehead.

"I didn't plan this relationship with Cassandra, Dorothy." Paul sounded defensive and paced around the room. "She was your best friend; then somehow she was my best friend. It just happened. Rob's hardly ever home. She's unhappy and wants to leave him." He paused. A small muscle twitched in his jaw as he turned to me without meeting my eyes.

"Look, I don't want to break up our home, and there are the kids to consider. I love you both. Why should I have to choose between you? Why not all live together? Cassandra's willing if you are."

"You want us all to live together?" I asked in a strangled little voice. My stomach lurched. It felt hard to breathe. The icepack slid to the floor as I sat up to stare at Paul in disbelief. "You mean like Mormons?"

I was crying hard. It crossed my mind that a three-way marriage would have been quite a happening in our social circle, but Paul, who I suspected had gone crazy in the throes of mid-life crisis , saw nothing strange about the idea.

I stared at him, speechless, while he attempted to sell me on this brave new venture. "Damn the conventions!" he declared. "I'm an Aquarian and ahead of my time. We could emulate those New Age thinkers out in California who're experimenting with multiple unions and take our relationship to a whole new level of intimacy. And, with more people in the marriage, everyone would have a greater chance to be happy!"

Paul's words horrified me—almost as much as the thought of divorcing him and raising two kids alone. The next morning, still weeping at Paul's betrayal, I packed up the kids and ran home to mother like a scared little girl—while Cassandra moved herself into my house to carry on our multiple union without me.

The kids and I spent two weeks with my mom in her city apartment, where she'd moved to be near her sister after my dad died. I slept beneath the furry pink bedspread I'd loved as a girl, with the framed unicorn poster from my old bedroom hanging on the wall— getting lots of rest while Grandma cared for the kids. She fed me chicken soup which was comforting, and hugged me reassuringly and smoothed back my hair like she did when I was little, but I could tell she was as frightened as I was that my marriage had fallen apart.

The only life for a woman she understood was being married and cared for by a husband. This was her life, until my dad's death when I was sixteen, and she was fifty-five. Now, at nearly seventy, she'd never recovered from the horror of his long illness and painful, untimely death. Her worn, lined face bore the imprint of the depression she'd suffered since then for which she took prescription tranquilizers.

"What will you do now, Dorothy?" she asked, as she helped me unpack. "An unfaithful husband is a huge betrayal of you and your marriage. Thankfully, your father was not only an excellent provider, but he was also a loyal and trustworthy marriage partner for twenty-five years until death did us part." My mom sighed, deeply, caught somewhere in her memories.

"Dorothy, honey, I can only imagine the pain you must feel. And while I agree your anger is justified...still," she paused to clear her throat, "No one in our family has ever been divorced—even your cousins, Bill and Betty, who really don't like each other. They still continue on as a couple for the sake of the children. Maybe you and Paul can still work things out..."

During my stay, I got out of bed long enough to seek counseling services, paid for by my mom— because, logic aside, I felt that everything that had happened was my fault.

If I'd only been more responsive in bed, Paul might not have strayed.

"What's wrong with me?" I wailed to the family counselor. "Nothing's wrong with you, lady," came the reply after hearing my story. "You're husband's a jerk. Get rid of him."

While I was gone, Cassandra moved herself into my house to stand at Paul's side—possibly affording many of my neighbors the first rush of high excitement they'd felt in years. Particularly, since her workaholic husband finally noticed she was missing and, I later learned, came by repeatedly to pound on the door and demand her return.

In the end, my mom did what she could for me. But aside from a generous check, which I felt guilty accepting, she had no practical advice to offer a woman in my situation.

Cassandra was gone when the boys and I returned home. I was still confused, but a step closer to knowing what to do about my life. I shared this knowledge with Paul the next morning after the kids left for school.

"You want a divorce?" Paul was examining his gray hairs in the bathroom mirror. He turned and stared at me, shocked.

"Yes, Paul, I do." My mom's words about divorce echoed in my mind, but I kept my voice steady.

"You're willing to throw away twelve years of marriage? Think of the children. Look, we could get a bigger house and live together—you, me, Cassandra, the kids. It would be great, Dorothy. Look, you're a Virgo," he said, sighing, "a conservative sign, can't you get past it and envision something greater?"

His words might have carried more weight if I hadn't just turned and noticed Cassandra's compact, lipstick, comb, and a small pile of hairpins, left behind on *my* nightstand. *Someone's been sleeping in my bed;* I thought and turned to face Paul again.

"We could all live together?" My voice rose up a notch with newfound strength. I was angry, angrier than I'd ever been in all my twenty-nine years. "In a little crooked house, no doubt, you son-of-a-bitch? And we'll feed you oysters every day so you can get it up when you play musical beds!"

We were screaming. Funny how when people live together for twelve years—if they learn nothing else about each other—they become adept at causing the other person the most emotional pain with the least possible effort.

Paul told me I was a rotten housekeeper, a lousy lay, and lowest of the low—a woman who couldn't hold her man.

I told him he was a liar, a cheat, and a deep disappointment. And that the aspiring writer I thought I was marrying had turned into an office manager with a family he resented and a mortgaged home in the suburbs. That shot hit home. He called me a frigid bitch, and I began throwing Cassandra's possessions in his direction.

"Get out! Get out get out get out, you cheating bastard! " I screamed.

Paul, crackling with anger, called me a frigid bitch once more with feeling. Then he stuffed his books and toiletries and favorite pieces of clothing into his battered brown suitcase, stomped out of the house, and went off to be with Cassandra, who understood him.

I spent the rest of that day crying, wondering how to explain to my sons that their father didn't live here anymore. Finally, after dinner, when it was almost dark outside, I couldn't put it off any longer. I called the kids in, sat them down on the couch, gathered them close, and informed them of our situation as honestly as I could.

"Your dad and I…well…we don't get along," I explained, lamely. "But I want you to understand that no matter what, your dad still loves you."

Brad, an Aquarian like his dad, didn't show his feelings much, but his deep brown eyes with their enigmatic expression, so like Paul's, widened with shock at my words. His mouth trembled slightly. Seeking comfort, he leaned closer to my side.

There was never a lot of doubt about what my little Gemini communicator, Doug, was thinking and feeling. His little face crumpled and his eyes pooled with tears. He climbed into my lap and snuggled while I kissed his soft cheek and stroked his shiny brown hair.

"Will everything be all right, Mom?" he asked, looking up at me. His high little voice was shaky. Brad looked on without speaking, waiting for my response.

Not knowing what else to do, I took a deep breath, lowered my voice at least an octave, and said as strongly as I could, "Don't worry guys. I'm here. Everything will be fine!"

Later, while my sons slept, I sat wide awake in the silent darkness staring out our front window at our small, neat yard with its white picket fence. And the newly single car parked in our driveway.

"Christ," I said aloud. "Whatever happened to happily ever after?"

Part Two—1975

Will You Marry Me?

CHAPTER TWO

Because we played that scene so well, we repeated it, even after we legally separated, while waiting for our divorce decree. We spent the summer apart and in the fall of 1974, Paul called, pleading to be taken back. He said Cassandra, now lived with a relative in Nevada and was out of the picture. Although I wasn't sure I forgave him, or trusted him, or liked him, I was scared to be alone—so in the name of the sanctity of marriage and family, we reunited. But only a month later I discovered a torrid love letter from Cassandra in Paul's sock drawer, revealing she was indeed still in the picture.

After playing one final round of *get out get out get out you cheating bastard!*—our marriage was done.

Now, at age thirty, I was hurt, angry, and felt terribly wronged by the institution of marriage and the society in which I lived, although I had trouble

23

pinpointing precisely how. True, I'd married young, with minimal dating experience and was a virgin until I began dating Paul. He was ten years my senior, with prior sexual experience. I imagined he knew more about sex than I did. When he told me I was frigid for not achieving vaginal orgasms, I believed him.

And in twelve years of marriage, I'd never once had an affair, and had produced two healthy sons. But sadly, whoever racked up the score had failed to record the points I'd earned, and I lost the game. How could this be? I believed with all my heart in happily ever after. I was a good girl. I was pretty. So what went wrong?

Maybe it was because I didn't know what "real life" was about or being an adult. Maybe it was because I grew up in the fabulous fifties and saw too many movies starring Doris Day, which always ended with blissful kisses and impending marriages.

My mom was against my marrying young and taking on adult responsibilities. "Don't rush into marriage," she urged. "Have fun first."

That should have told me there wouldn't be much fun afterward.

I wondered what happened to Doris when the movie ended. Was it diaper pails and bills and fun on special occasions only? I wanted to know because that's what happened to me. And I was as good-looking as she was, just as sweet and bright and funny. There I was ready for bliss everlasting, and what happened? I got a husband who wanted a second wife without leaving his first one. Doris always got Rock Hudson or Cary Grant. And once married, did the happy couple enjoy a grand old sex life? Well hell yes! Who could imagine well balanced Doris going to sleep high and dry?

I knew all about high and dry. Had anyone inquired about my sex life with Paul, I could sum it up by saying: I had sex after the eleven o'clock news—quickies mostly, what with work the next day and kids to care for. The eleven o'clock news came first. I came (when I came) after.

However it happened, facts were facts. Till death-do-us-part had come to a screeching halt—and Paul quit his job and moved to Nevada with Cassandra, before the issue of child support was fully discussed. "I'm going to write an astrology book," he said. "I'll send money when I can."

This information came in a brief, judgmental note in which Paul expressed love and concern for his sons. It ended with, "I took care of my family for twelve years. Cassandra feels she owes it to the world to nurture my talents as an astrologer. She will support me while I make my contribution to mankind."

I was womankind; he planned to contribute nothing to me.

I took Paul's letter to the local social services office. The address was a post office box in Reno Nevada. "He refused to pay child support. Maybe you could track him down and have him arrested," I suggested, but they weren't interested.

"Nevada's a non-reciprocal state," the social services lady said, shrugging her shoulders. "They don't share information with other states. He's pretty well untouchable, even if we had his home address. Sorry."

Oh God, I thought, *not only will I die of loneliness; I'm going to starve to death too. This kind of thing never ever happened to Doris Day.*

My new life was filled with major issues for me to confront. The biggest was being a single mom. No matter what, life with kids went on as always. I cooked their meals, made their school lunches, cleaned their rooms, and washed their clothes. I played scrabble with Brad and Old Maid with Doug. I helped them with homework (unless it was math) and broke up their endless arguments when it sounded like a life was in danger. I quickly discovered I wasn't much of an authority figure. I'd been the fun parent, almost a kid myself. When Paul told the boys no, it was no. When I told them no, it was up for debate.

I was a mom, but I was a single woman too. I wasn't unwilling to adjust to being one; the problem was I'd never been alone in my life and simply didn't know how. Everyone said not to worry because I was young with a long life ahead of me and someday I'd look back on all this and laugh. But I didn't believe them. My life was my life with Paul, and now it was over. I felt disoriented and confused and unbearably alone—like a Siamese twin after surgery, free at last and wondering *oh my god what do I do now?*

"Help," I said aloud. *I need a basic survival course. One I should have taken years ago. Why don't the universities teach something useful like Single Woman 101: How to Cope When You're Hurting, or, Money Management for the Newly-Separated Woman with No Money, No Job, and No Work Experience?*

Help!

Aside from financial help from my mom, along with home-baked cookies and clothes for the kids, the practical help I got came from my new neighbor across the street. Carla Page was a six-foot-tall, curvy, dark-haired, Aquarian woman with a wicked sense of humor. At thirty-eight she had two young boys and a sweet, dependable Capricorn husband named Ray, who owned the local hardware store and provided well for his family.

Carla became my best friend, watched my kids when I couldn't afford a sitter, gave me moral support when I most needed it, and even on occasion made me laugh—which serves to prove that behind every successful woman is another woman.

We met in a supermarket a week after my initial separation. I was attempting to purchase food but instead wandered aimlessly, feeling like a stranger in an alien land among the local housewives, food-shopping for their husbands—who, unlike mine, would be home for dinner.

Carla found me looking depressed in the cheese section. Being a neighbor, she'd heard about the comings and goings at my house and that Paul had moved out. When she asked, kindly, if I was okay, I told her I was getting divorced and to my horror, began sobbing uncontrollably.

"Come on," she said and took me home with her for a visit.

We sat in my new friend's blue and white kitchen, drinking coffee and talking for hours. Well, she talked, I cried. I must have been miserable company, but lucky me, Carla's the type who takes in stray puppies and other small lost critters, so I had a friend. What a relief to have someone to talk to and help me figure things out.

"My life's a mess," I wailed. "What's wrong with me?"

Carla set down her cup, looked at me, and sighed. "In my twenties," she said, "before Ray, I was married to a successful man I tried hard to satisfy. I shopped, cooked, decorated, and entertained when he wanted me to. I spent a small fortune on beauty products so I'd look good on his arm at social functions. I put off having kids—what I wanted most—because he liked to party and didn't want to be tied down. He eventually put me out of my misery by divorcing me so he could marry his lovely, young secretary who was pregnant with his child."

She grinned and poured more coffee. "I felt as

you do, that my marriage failed because *I* wasn't perfect enough, and beat myself up over it—until I decided that was garbage and began building a new life."

"But I feel like my life is over," I said.

Carla shrugged. "One part is over, and a new part begins. And this time around, *you'll* write the rules. It's 1975. We've come a long way, baby, since getting the vote."

I stared at her, feeling the first rush of hope since Paul left home. *She's been scared and alone, too. Maybe cried at night, like I do, for someone to hold her and say I love you, and make everything all right. Look at her now: a loving, second husband, two happy kids. She's confident and secure. Maybe I'll feel that way, too.*

"The first thing you need to do is talk to a lawyer and get the house in your name only," Carla said. "Ray knows someone; I'll get you his name." She continued her pep talk. "And now that you're single, Dorothy, you may want to start dating. I'll bet you haven't dated since you were seventeen." She flashed me an encouraging smile. I smiled at Brad like that on his first day of kindergarten.

"Who am I going to date? I don't know any men." I was crying again.

"You'll meet men at work," she assured me. "You'll be getting a job, won't you?"

"A job?" Oh god, she was right! Someone had to make the mortgage payments, buy the food, and keep the boys in sneakers. Brad turned twelve in February and Doug wasn't quite eight. Someone had to do these things for *years*. "Who's going to take care of us?" I asked.

Carla raised her eyebrows. Rolled her eyes. "My guess is you are. I see no other choice."

She had a point. "I'll get a job!" I decided, with my Virgo tenacity. "At least until Prince Charming shows up to take over."

But a job doing what? I wondered. I can make ceramic sculptures that my college professors said showed real talent. I did well in all my art classes, know a lot about kids, a little about astrology, and am reasonably well read. Besides this, I'm smart, sensitive and funny—and armed with these formidable qualifications, I will march out into the world and take it by storm.

Reaching for Carla's newspaper, I opened it to the women's section of the want ads and went down the list: bartender, bank teller, secretary, typist, waitress; experience a must." Surely there's something..." I finished reading and set the paper down.

"There's nothing I qualify for...I'm an artist..." My voice was tiny. "Oh Carla, what am I going to do?" I was crying again. Now there was something I was good at—but was it a marketable skill?

"There are job openings for typists."

"But I can't type!"

Carla's patience was wearing thin. "Dorothy, face it; you're in a tough situation. You're on your own with two kids who are counting on you to support them. Sink or swim—those are your choices. I'd learn to type if I were you."

"Sink or swim. Sink or swim." I mumbled under my breath all the way to the typing school downtown. I enrolled myself and pecked away at the keyboard, thinking that never, as a little girl, did I say one word to anyone about wanting to be a typist when I grew up.

By the time I'd worked up to twenty-six words a minute, I found a job at the Foxy Lady Niteclub where—*I am woman, I am strong*—I was hired because I was pretty.

Being a nightclub hostess, I was told, comes under the heading of a glamour job. For the record, this isn't true. My job interview was interesting, though. Turns out the boss was a Scorpio, which rules sexuality. True to his sign he oozed sex from every pore. His look told me I turned him on; my long, curling hair was beautiful, my body belonged in Playboy, and that I had bedroom eyes. He inspected me so closely, in fact, I wondered if he'd open my mouth, like they do with horses, and check my teeth—although I suspected teeth weren't his primary interest.

So, I was hired because I was pretty and because my boss felt my art background might enable me to hand people their menus in some creative way. Still, the job paid almost enough to live on, and I got to walk around in a slinky dress and look seductive as I showed customers to their tables. I found the nightlife at the Foxy Lady fascinating, and the most nightlife I'd seen so far. The new vibration excited me. Conversing with men excited me too, and seeing the desire in their eyes.

I asked most men I met their zodiac signs and true to my sign began analyzing the information given. (I did this because I imagined it would be easier to find the perfect man for me if I could first determine that perfect man's zodiac sign.) That's how I become the only nightclub hostess in Syracuse New York who knew or cared, if the patrons of the Foxy Lady Niteclub were Virgos, Pieces, or Leos.

Winter was finally over. No more snow. April was rainy but mild; plants began to flower and leaves appeared on the trees. Life looked brighter. I worked evenings. Carla watched the kids, so I didn't have to squeeze the cost of a sitter from my tiny salary. I smiled more often and felt okay as long as I was with other people. At home, I held myself together when the boys were around, but the minute I was alone, I disintegrated and rushed to Carla for moral support.

"What would I do without you?" I asked, feeling grateful for her friendship and humiliated by my inability to function alone.

"Been there myself, kid." she said, "I'll speak up when I'm sick of you. Besides, you're coming along. Yesterday you didn't cry all afternoon. And you made a joke. It was funny."

I was coming along—a swimmer after all. I squared my shoulders. My spirits lifted. Then the creditors began to call.

"Mrs. Freed? This is Mr. Gallipoli from Fourth National Bank, calling about your charge card. It seems you owe us five-thousand-eight-hundred-eighty dollars, and sixty-two cents. Our records show no payment from you since March."

That made sense. March was when Cassandra Charming carried Paul off to the wild, wild west to support his literary endeavors, and where he'd never work another day in his life.

"I'm sure this is a misunderstanding," Mr. Gallipoli continued, "but unless we receive back payments of nine-hundred-fifty-four dollars and sixteen cents within five business days, we'll be forced to turn your account over to a collection agency. Now I know you don't want that to happen."

"There must be some mistake," I said. "I've never made a credit card purchase; never even carried one in my wallet. My husband handled financial matters, and he's moved across country."

"Your name is on the card," Mr. Gallipoli said flatly, "you are equally responsible under the law."

I was stunned. The knowledge that I was being held liable for thousands of dollars of debt went straight to my stomach and stayed there like a lead weight.

"Look, I've just started working. I earn barely enough to make ends meet. My mom sends me money to pick up the slack." My voice got shaky as I tried to make this nice man understand. "You see Paul cheated on me and..." I bored Mr. Gallipoli with the sad story of my life until he interrupted to request my payment again, and I hung up on him.

I ran to Carla with my latest tale of woe. She listened and hugged me, but there wasn't much more she could do. My personal problems didn't interest the folks at Fourth National. Paul was off fulfilling his creative potential, while I was here within easy reach.

Oh God, two kids, and no money. I could skip town, I thought, wildly. But I couldn't afford that either. Besides, I had nowhere to go.

Creditors continued to call leaving me trembling, fearing they'd put a lien on my house. It was mine now according to our divorce agreement, uncontested by Paul, payment-in-full for twelve years of being a wife. It was mortgaged to the hilt, and in need of repair, but to me, that house was the light at the end of the long dark tunnel that was now my life. Someday, when I found someplace to go, I'd sell it and use the tiny profit to start over. There wasn't enough to share.

I thought my situation over carefully, having been raised to be honest and to honor my obligations. Then I calculated that at my present salary, I could afford to give my creditors about fourteen dollars a month for the rest of my life—which I offered them, but they said no.

Carla said I was coming along, learning to roll

with the punches, and maybe so. I'd always been a worrier, and for most of my life constantly worried about all sorts of small things. Now, I only worried about one big thing, *basic survival.* With life moving faster by the day I found less time for crying and began feeling flashes of optimism about making a new life.

While I stalled creditors and searched for a better paying job, I felt painfully alone. Aside from my kids and occasional visits from my mom, I spent my free time with Carla, thinking up schemes for escape, and envying the paycheck Ray brought home to her each week.

When Carla and Ray went out on the town, they often invited me along. I accepted their invitations gratefully, but at the end of the evening, after they'd gone home together, I ached with loneliness and cried myself to sleep.

My first affair was with a businessman I met at the Foxy Lady after working there two months. Dating customers was out, but I didn't ask permission. As a man and a lover, he had two qualifications: he was male, and he wanted me. And how I wanted a man to want me, to assure me I was desirable—to validate me like a parking sticker, to give me an orgasm like a Christmas gift. So I could say, "Screw you, Paul, there's nothing wrong with me."

So the first man to ask got the prize; my virginity the second time around. It was a brief affair, a few movies and meals and maybe an hour in bed—plus several faked orgasms to show what a dynamite hunk of woman I was. What I remember most is he couldn't find my clit and I was too shy to direct him. His penis was arc-shaped and shorter than Paul's.

My mom would disagree, but the affair provided me an opportunity to feel beautiful, seductive, and powerful for a little while. Besides, I believed I needed a new husband to make a good life.

All I had to do, I decided, was go out and find him.

Perfect Stranger Encounter #1

James

The jukebox was on full volume when I entered the Purple Rooster Niteclub. Kris Kristofferson's soft, sexy voice beseeched me to help him make it through the night. They're playing my song, I thought and caught the blind eye of a massive wooden rooster, purple, like everything else in the club. "Hello," I told the bird, "this must be the place for the manhunt." I looked around, uneasily. I'd agonized for hours about what to wear—finally choosing skin tight jeans and a clingy top to show off my petite, hour-glass figure. I completed my outfit with my highest pair of heels—and slipped my diaphragm, in its plastic container into my evening bag, so please, god, if I did get laid I wouldn't get pregnant. Then, I argued with myself before leaving home.

Carla, bless her, kept an eye out for the kids, and Ray said if I ran into problems, to call him and he'd come to pick me up.

Now, that I was here my stomach was doing flip-flops. Feeling insecure, I hesitated over where to sit. At the bar, I might appear obvious in my intention—but at a dimly-lit table, I might be ignored, which would be worse. I climbed onto a barstool and watched a stream of happy looking people pass by. Then I zoomed in for a closer look, at the women in particular.

Hey, blonde lady, in form-fitting black with your well-dressed date at your side; is it true you have more fun? Or you, in the pantsuit, looking like you stepped out of Cosmo? How passionate are your nights? Do you laugh? Do you love? Do you come? No one answered my unspoken questions. They walked on by, smiling, two by two—and I was all alone on Noah's Ark.

I felt the man in the sports jacket watching me before I saw him. Handsome guy; with a dimple on his chin like Kirk Douglas. I stared at him, then felt flustered and almost looked away. *Come on, Dorothy, the man wants to meet you. This is why you're here, isn't it dear? Or would you prefer to go home and watch late-night TV again? Yes, my eyes told him. Let's meet, and you'll be my boyfriend and wine and dine me, and think I'm wonderful because you see the inner me. And you'll love my sons as your own, take them to ballgames and do guy stuff with them. Oh, and by the way, will you marry me?* The man was at my side, smiling like he'd found buried treasure.

"I've been watching you, thinking; what a pretty woman. I wonder if she's alone."

"She is," I said, "all alone."

"Well, that's easily remedied." He smiled and slid smoothly onto the stool beside me, setting his pack of Marlboros and lighter on the bar, beside my glass and evening purse. "Care for another drink?"

I hesitated. The ginger ale I was drinking didn't fit my sexy image. My mind blanked as I tried to think of a sophisticated drink to order. What was it Carla liked? "Bourbon over ice," I said.

Our drinks arrived. We sipped and made small talk. I was so nervous I almost choked on my bourbon but managed to control myself as the seduction went on.

My new friend, James was a Leo, wide-shouldered and slim-waisted, with high cheekbones and a captivating smile "Shall we dance?" He got to his feet and extended a hand.

I hesitated. I loved dancing but hadn't in years. Paul didn't dance, considered it overrated foreplay. Wouldn't want too much of that clogging up our marriage, now would we?

"Yes," I said, hoping I wouldn't step all over him, or look like a fool, or…

Dancing made me feel wilder than the wind and movie star desirable. My eyes were half-closed as I lost myself in the sound and movement. Not too lost though, to notice heads turn to watch me, or the man's look of admiration at the slow, sensuous movements of my body.

"You're a great dancer," James said when the song ended, and we'd returned to our seats.

"Am I really?" I asked, gazing into his eyes.

"You are, really." His eyes explored my body. "Are you divorced?" he asked. His arm slipped around my shoulders. It felt good. I let it stay where it was.

"Practically, it'll be final in the fall. And you?"

"Divorced. Isn't everyone?" he asked, laughing.

"I'm beginning to think so," I said. "What ever happened to happily ever after?"

He smiled, appreciating my wit, although I hadn't meant to be funny. His weight shifted slightly, so the hardness of this thigh pressed against mine. I could feel his body heat through his clothes and didn't move away.

"Happily ever after could begin right now," he said. "Do you know you have the largest, most beautiful green eyes I've ever seen?"

He was really turned on by me. I could feel his attraction. Smiling a thank you, my mind moved beyond the moment and I visualized us walking through life hand in hand, with long nights of lovemaking and picnics on the beach with the kids. He said he loved kids. *Carla, I want you to meet my new boyfriend, James. I orgasm every time we have sex.*

"Sorry," I said, realizing James was speaking to me. "What did you say?"

"Could we go somewhere quieter?"

"Where could we go?" I asked. But of course, I already knew.

So, Dorothy, the offer of the evening is sex with a perfect stranger. Is that what I want? I could go home. But home is two sleeping children and a dark, quiet neighborhood—and being alone. And this man is so attractive, so masculine, so warm and alive. His eyes are clear, bright blue. Maybe he'll love me and change my life by proving that Prince Charming lives, after all.

Let me stick out my foot. Try on the glass slipper.

"Will you come to my place?" he asked standing, smiling down at me, and extending his hand.

Yes," I said, feeling swept away by desire and wanting to yield to him. I rose to join him, and we were on our way.

From the bar to the car to the bed in that much talked about twinkle of an eye. James lived downtown near the library. I felt surprisingly at ease in his wood-paneled bedroom, doing a slow striptease, while he watched my every move with lust in his eyes. When I was naked, he swept me into his arms like he'd waited years to hold me. I pressed my face to his chest. He smelled of soap and sweat and intoxicating maleness. His breathing quickened. His mouth met mine. I felt like I was doing a scene from *Gone with the Wind.*

I wish I could say I had multiple orgasms that night, but I didn't...I got pretty aroused when James went down on me. His hot, wet tongue felt so good my groin was alive with sensation. I thought I could come, but he didn't quite hit the right spot, and then stopped before I could think how to show him and wanted me to reciprocate. His cock was veiny and quite thick. I sucked it until my jaws ached while wondering if he liked me. Whether he did or not, he was clearly impressed with my performance.

"Baby, you're fantastic! Your husband was nuts to let you go. You came like crazy," he said, "three or four times, at least, didn't you?"

I hesitated; longing to be truthful but fearful of turning him off if I did. Men liked women who had vaginal orgasms—wasn't Paul proof of that? I faked a satisfied smile. "I lost count," I said, and he took me in his arms. Basking in his approval, I wondered why I suddenly disliked both of us so much.

But still, there we were, feeling almost like friends, as we sat talking after sex before he saw me to my car in the small hours of the morning. We discussed how Paul never saw me as an equal adult, and how his ex-wife, Amy, never had an orgasm in their entire seven years together. He'd tried everything he could think of. Nothing worked. He'd really suffered over that.

We discussed our kids, his two girls, my two boys, and his high-powered position with an ad agency. Maybe he could help me get a job.

"Goodnight. You're nothing less than wonderful," he said, and kissed me, tenderly, before I got in my car. I thought he might ask me out again before we parted, but he didn't. He had my phone number though and liked me so much I felt certain he'd call. I kissed him once more before driving home, where, buoyant with excitement, I floated to my room and to sleep.

The next day I floated to Carla's house to tell her I'd met a great looking, eligible guy who really liked me, and was going to call me, and spend time with me, and I'd have a steady boyfriend.

I never saw James again. I waited two weeks for his phone call before realizing I was a one night stand.

Perfect Strangers

CHAPTER THREE

Life was a drag. I worked nights, worried days, and on my nights off while my sons slept, searched for someone to love me. I tried to be strong, so they'd feel secure, but they sensed our precarious position and expressed their confusion in ways that kids do. Doug's teacher called to say he was disruptive in class, would I speak to him? Brad, usually an easygoing kid, got into two fights in one week. His math teacher informed me his grades had gone down and that he'd talked back to her when she'd spoken to him about it.

Why shouldn't they be upset? I thought, aching for them—with their father off on his mid-life adventure and their mom working and worrying about money all the time. But they were children after all. They played. They fought. They were hard to handle. The need to be mother and father to them felt overwhelming.

Sink or swim. The structure of my life has changed. I have to adapt to it.

Turns out, changing and adapting are easier said than done. I was sitting alone at my kitchen table one evening. Carla was on her break from helping me cope with my life and was home with her family. Brad and Doug were in the living room screaming at each other.

"You lost my baseball! What did you do with it?"

"I never touched your crummy ball!"

"Yes, you did! I saw you with it yesterday."

"It was mine anyway! I just let you use it."

"Give it to me now, or I'll step on your head!"

"Owwww!" There was the sound of crying. "MOM! Brad hit me! MOM!"

"I'm going to go crazy," I said aloud. "Men in white coats will come and take me away from all this, to a lovely padded cell where I can rest and have carefully selected visitors."

Reluctantly, I got up, intending to handle the situation, when the phone rang. Maybe a single man saw me somewhere yesterday and spent the last twenty-four hours tracking me down. Maybe he's calling to invite me to dinner. Maybe...

"Hello," I purred into the phone.

The man at the other end of the line was a creditor. "Mrs. Freed," he began, "I'm calling about your delinquent credit card payment of..."

"Look," I interrupted, "why don't you track my husband down and have him arrested. He quit working, moved across country, and left me with two children and no child support. I have no money. Leave me alone!" Tears poured from my eyes, and I hung up the phone.

"MOM!" Doug was screaming. "MOM! Brad kicked me!"

Later, at a bar, I drowned my sorrows in a Cancer with large liquid eyes. I forgot his name an hour after meeting him, but went home with him anyway, because I didn't want to be alone. The man went down on me, but although he tried hard failed to make me come, so I faked it. I didn't see him again, even though he asked for my number, and said I had the most beautiful green eyes he'd ever seen.

While waiting for life to improve, I spent my time caring for the kids, working, and playing around. A big change from before, when I didn't work outside my home, taking care of the kids *was* my job, and all my free time was spent molding lumps of clay.

Sometimes I found myself standing in my "studio" gazing at my work table, aching for the moist pliant feel of the clay, and the excitement of taking it in my hands and transforming it. But with my life in a constant state of upheaval, I lacked the will to work. I felt like a lump of clay myself—formless and indistinct, waiting to be molded into some clear and definite shape.

And I want to have fun. To take up where I left off at seventeen when I married Paul and began being an adult. I want to date, flirt, and play; to be admired, courted, and seduced. But most of all, I want a new husband to replace the old one.

Damn it! I wanted another crack at happily ever after!

I found a new bar and a new boyfriend, a Pisces

this time, who wined and dined me. He loved going down, found my clitoris, sucked it right, and Bingo! I had an orgasm. I thought I was in love.

Carla was unimpressed. "Dorothy, you met him last week. Go easy with the relationships. Give yourself time to gain experience."

She kept talking, but I was lost in a fantasy. The new man was good-looking, well-off, and skilled at lovemaking. With luck, he could handle the children, provide me with security, and hang up on the creditors. I couldn't understand why Carla wasn't pleased. The fantasy was short lived. I soon discovered the man had a drinking problem and four ex-wives.

My next three boyfriends—can you believe it?—were all married men who wanted to play. I began to feel angry. I was ready to give all of myself. What a rude awakening to realize how little of me they wanted.

"Carla, what's going on? No wonder Diogenes ran around searching for an honest man. I think I'll join him! Can't these men warn a person that they drink like fish, or they're cheating on their wives, or that they have nine children they forgot to mention? I'm not good at dating. I meet a man, and he seems like everything I want. Then I find the fatal flaw."

Carla shook her head and gave me a look. "Trust me," she said, "you need to know a man longer than five minutes before deciding he's Prince Charming."

The men I dated over the next several months each came with his own set of quirks and peculiarities.

The ceramics professor was kind, intelligent, and made wonderful, finely crafted, porcelain bowls, but was paranoid about germs and wouldn't go down on me. No hidden wives or children, but in his case, it didn't matter. The next man was single with strong male energy but was more energetic than imaginative in bed. The restaurant owner who followed seemed perfect for me, but let it slip a week later that his wife didn't understand him.

I told him goodbye and cursed all men—but even as I did this my eyes were wide open, looking to see who was next. There was a curiosity now, about cocks and other pleasurable playthings, as I realized that men came in an interesting variety of shapes and sizes.

I began to wonder about the astrological correlations.

The weeks passed, and I adjusted to the new tempo of my life, thinking my major traumas were over. I got a raise at work, which pleased me until I opened my mail and discovered a collection agency was garnishing my wages and suing for a lien on my house.

"I'm screwed," I told Carla. "I won't see a dime if I sell it, and if I don't, I'll be stuck in a dead-end job, paying off creditors."

My heart pounded. The prospect of spending the next thirty years at the Foxy Lady Niteclub rose before me like a monster in a horror film. I almost cried but changed my mind.

"Damn it!" I shouted, "This isn't fair, and I

refuse to let this happen to me!"

Suddenly, I knew what I needed to do. It was nothing my mom ever taught me. "It's so simple," I said. "Sell the house, take the money, and split."

Carla stared at me a moment, then her face broke into a big broad smile. "I think you could pull it off, Dorothy," she said, nodding her head, "if you move fast enough."

My decision made, I contacted the collection agency with stories, designed to buy time. The rules of the game were simple: lie, stall, and evade. The realtor said the house should move quickly if I were willing to sell cheap, and I was. What I needed next was someplace to go.

I was becoming cynical about real life. It wasn't enough like a Hollywood script to suit me. I don't mean a Doris Day script either—like the one where Cary Grant's block-long limo splashes mud on her dress, and they end up married. I mean more like Ellen Burstyn, in *Alice Doesn't Live Here Anymore*. That's the one about a single mom and her kid, on their own in the world for about *five minutes*, with the mom dreaming of making it as a singer—until she meets a handsome, single, affluent rancher played by Kris Kristofferson. He falls for her on sight and tenderly cultivates her friendship until she agrees to marry him and live happily ever after. Nice for Ellen. But where's *my* handsome, affluent single guy? All I'm meeting are sex-crazed fools who can't remember they're married. Damn! Someone swiped my Hollywood ending.

My divorce, which became final in late October, shook me up more than anticipated. I felt unbearably alone that night in my quiet house. My kids were asleep, and I sat on the sofa recalling scenes from my marriage until I couldn't take anymore. I called Carla, who said she'd look out for the kids. Then I put on makeup, skintight black bellbottoms, and went out hunting.

Part of me felt wild and free, as I walked out the front door. "Let's get laid!" that wild part said, while a more timid, introverted part of me went hesitantly along for the ride—hoping against hope I'd find someone out there to love me so all my troubles would end.

But the next morning, I was terribly upset. Single life wasn't working out. I longed for love and instead, all I was getting was screwed. I wondered what went wrong. I was pretty; with small, perky breasts, clear, smooth skin, and a body that made men drool. Wasn't it written that unhappiness came only to unattractive women? DAMN! Twelve years of marriage and true love was still light years away. I didn't make it married. Now I had problems being single.

After the boys left for school, I sat at my kitchen table mulling it over, remembering the men I'd had sex with since splitting with Paul. Perfect strangers all of them—until I took that fatal closer look, and saw they weren't so perfect after all: like the businessman, who talked a future, but wanted just one night. Or the writer who said the age of commitment was dead. Or the musician who entered my life one horny evening and left it forever before morning came.

Midnight cowboys, come for midnight rides...

I looked back in anger at all of them. As their images came to mind, they blurred, and merged, into a spinning wheel of naked strangers. I wondered how many there were and began making a list, feeling powerful as I reduced each man to a name a number and a zodiac sign. Well, I thought when I finished, it's a spinning wheel all right, but from now on, *I'll* do the spinning. Around and around she goes, where she stops nobody knows. Like Scarlett O'Hara, who'll never be hungry again, I'll never be hurt or lonely again. Frankly, my dear, I don't give a damn, either!

There was too, a particular intense excitement in being alone in a room with a perfect stranger, with nothing between us but sex. Since the perfect marriage had eluded me, I might as well go for the intense excitement—with maybe a perfect vaginal orgasm or two to be had in the bargain.

I was relieved to finally understand how to deal with men. I would do unto them as they did to me. No more hoping they'd like me, praying they'd love me or waiting for one of them to look close enough to see me, hiding, in the depths of my beautiful green eyes. Okay, Dorothy, you've got the idea now. Welcome to the seventies, girl, and off down the Yellow Brick Road you go.

Libra, Pisces and Cancer, oh my!

Life Plan: I wrote on a fresh sheet of paper, sell house, skip town, get job; screw everyone.

I was planning out a study of the sexual habits of a whole lot of men when a miracle happened, and Carla rushed in, all excited.

"Dorothy! How would you like to move to San Francisco?"

"San Francisco," I repeated, looking around my kitchen. One window was broken; I'd have to replace it before winter. The linoleum was worn, and the back door had warped and wouldn't shut properly. Brad and his friends had smashed a sizable hole in the wall in some improbable accident with a hardball. Now I didn't need to look out the window to watch him play in the yard. The letter on my Formica kitchen table informed me that a lien was being filed on my house, for my failure make back payments of two thousand, eight-hundred-fifty-dollars, and thirty-four cents. And, there was a note from my realtor saying he'd received a lowball offer on the house, would I care to accept it?

"We can leave next month," I said. "What do I do when we get there?"

Carla explained: Ray's old pal in San Francisco knew a businessman who was opening a coffeehouse/art gallery in the Haight-Ashbury, and was seeking a manager with an art background. "Here's the number," she said, "call the guy, talk to him."

I called and ten minutes later had a job, which included an apartment behind the coffee house. I hugged Carla, dancing her around the room. We were on our way!

As a swan song to my old life, I went on one grand sexual binge before leaving—marching through town like Sherman through Atlanta—laying flat every man in my path: Hal owned the gas station that serviced my car. Bill was a therapist I met through a friend. Arnie was Brad's sixth-grade teacher. Jacob owned a local bar.

I couldn't wait to leave town.

The house sold quickly. My mom was shocked and scandalized to learn what her daughter was doing— "Leaving town like a thief in the night," she said—but I felt like the proverbial million dollars. I hadn't wanted to cheat anyone but didn't see a more appealing choice. I now understood that my sons and I would survive in this world by my wits and determination—a whole new worldview. *Look at me, Carla. I can swim!*

"Are you scared, Mom?" Brad asked, the night before we moved. We were camped out in Carla's living room. Doug snored softly in a sleeping bag near the front window. "Are you?" he repeated.

My arm went around his shoulders. "Scared to death," I said, "but that won't stop me."

My son stared at me, big-eyed. "I have faith in you, Mom," he said, with twelve-year-old wisdom, and kissed me goodnight.

I lay on Carla's sofa trying to sleep, but my mind raced with thoughts of San Francisco, that city of freedom that all those kids kept running to during the Summer of Love, the year Doug was born; the city I'd heard so much about—where no matter what your thing was, you could find somewhere to do it and someone to do it with. It was the perfect place for me to start over.

"Relax," Carla said the next morning as we loaded the last of my possessions into Big Bertha, our ancient station wagon.

"Right," I agreed, fretting about the move, and how the boys would adjust to big city life, and their new schools. I was excited and anxious to be gone and terrified and unsure I wanted to go. My stomach was leaping around inside me by the time Bertha was ready to roll.

"Ready or not, here we go," I said, and the two of us stood looking at each other. "I'll miss you." Carla sounded sad. There were tears in her eyes.

"How will you possibly manage without me and my problems?" I joked, as my tears started. We exchanged looks, one woman to another. "Thank you so much for everything," I sobbed.

Carla's arms went around me. We hugged, "I gave you pointers, Dorothy. You did the rest." She grinned. "Hell, I know a swimmer when I see one."

Tears were running down my face as I herded the boys to the car. Turning, I looked back at the house I'd called home for many years and all but drowned in a flood of memories.

"Let's go already, Mom!" Brad and Doug were yelling. "Goodbye. Goodbye."

"I know you'll make a good life," Carla whispered, "Call when you get there, so I'll know you're safe. And write soon and often."

"I will," I promised, getting in the car. I turned the ignition key. Big Bertha coughed to life, and I was on my way.

Go west, young woman.

Part Three—1976

Libra And Pisces And Cancer, Oh My!

CHAPTER FOUR

I escaped to San Francisco on a cold, mid-October morning, in 1975. The world felt fresh and full of possibilities as I sat in the driver's seat heading my family due west. Being in charge felt good to me; I'd always been relegated to the passenger seat in my travels with Paul, and I felt a greater sense of freedom with each passing mile. It took ten days for us to travel across country, stopping at scenic spots along the way.

I couldn't stop smiling as I drove into San Francisco. Doug was whining, "When are we going to get there, Mom?" And Brad was grousing because we'd crossed the Bay Bridge instead of the Golden Gate. But I had no complaints. From the moment I saw my new city, it was love at first sight. For the first time in my life, I was home.

Driving up Haight Street, there was so much to see, I almost ran us up onto the sidewalk about seven times per block. I couldn't take my eyes off the brightly painted Victorian houses with their bay windows crowded with potted plants. Or the brightly colored people, of all ages, all races, who walked unhurriedly—like they had all the time in the world—along the sunny street.

We stopped for a red light at the famous corner of Haight and Ashbury. I gawked at a stocky man in a fringed leather vest, with Jesus-like hair and beard. He passed a lit joint to a scrawny blond in a purple dress and silver bracelets above her elbows. Near them, an obese, redheaded woman wore what appeared to be a tie-dyed tent, in rainbow colors. She carried an enormous iguana in her arms and was singing an aria from *Carmen* at the top of her lungs. No one gawked or appeared to find them unusual in any way.

"Well, boys," I said, "I've got a feeling we're not in upstate New York anymore."

My boss, Mr. Conklin, was sixtyish, decked out in multi-colored batik, a sharks' tooth necklace, and wore an abundance of Patchouli oil. He welcomed us at the door, resembling a middle-aged businessman masquerading as a cool person. (Another erotic fantasy of mine shot to hell.)

The boys regarded him with suspicion as we went inside. "You look way too young to have such big boys." he gushed, patting Doug's head. Doug snarled, and I flashed him a warning look.

"This is the coffee house," he said, with a wave of his hand, indicating a large dim room with a bay window looking out onto Haight Street, near Golden Gate Park. Old wooden tables and chairs dotted the place, with a sink, espresso machine, and storage shelves behind the counter at the back of the room. Paintings depicting fruit bowls, flower-filled vases, and formal looking women in gowns posing on couches, lined the walls. Mr. Conklin and his wife, Milly, the painter, hoped to turn the place into a flourishing art gallery.

Windows need washing, I noted, looking around—and plants; lots of them, and way fewer paintings. Our apartment was at the back of the building, connected to the coffeehouse by a dark paneled hallway. Mr. Conklin showed us around, handed me the keys, and went home. The place would open in two weeks. We had time to settle in.

I surveyed my new home. It's no fantasy apartment, I thought: walls need painting, floors need scraping, and the furnishings have been around since the ice age at least. But there are two decent-sized bedrooms and a kitchen that will get morning sun, and with some paint, fabric and *lots* of labor, that ugly living room has possibilities. And I'm in San Francisco, only blocks from the famous corner of Haight and Ashbury, with a whole new life ahead of me, and no husband telling me what to do. No creditors calling either and many new men to meet. I eyed my new bed speculatively.

I went to check on Brad and Doug, who were in their bedroom arguing over who was going to sleep in the top bunk bed.

"I'll only sleep on top if I get the big dresser!" Doug shrieked.

"I'm older. I have more clothes!" Brad yelled back.

"Mom!" they both shouted when they saw me, but I sidestepped the issue and threw my arms around them. "Hey guys" I exulted, "we're home!"

Dear Carla,

Just a note to let you know I'm alive and well and living in the Land of Oz—otherwise known as San Francisco. Since arriving here last month, I've been out and about exploring this enchanting city. And it's cool, far out, and mellow, man, mellow. I dig it!

San Francisco is color and costume, and women who don't shave under their arms, and wear mood rings, and earrings in their noses. Its natural food, and alfalfa sprouts, and grass, and psychics, and people who are gay and proud of it. And freedom for all who claim it!

It's the freedom part I like best, Carla. No doubt about it, this is the place for that. I'm a long way from the suburbs of Syracuse New York in every way, with no one to tell me I'm wrong, or weird, or crazy, or what's the "right" way to think and feel.

Actually, even if I was wrong or weird or crazy, I'd doubt anybody here would notice, or even care, since everyone is busy doing their own thing, whether it appears to make sense or not. I'm planning to do my own thing too—as soon as I determine what that thing is.

Seriously, now that I've had time to think things over, I've drawn some conclusions about life. My main conclusion is that the world is basically insane. Fool that I am, I didn't know this, and most of my troubles were caused by my stubborn insistence that life should make sense. I know better now: a person exhibiting sane behavior in an insane world is destined to get trounced.

I don't propose to get trounced anymore, Carla. I propose to have a lot of fun. It's occurred to me that I've spent most of my life restraining my natural impulses. Now, like Lincoln freeing the slaves, I'm turning those impulses loose. I'm planning to try it all!

There are plenty of men around now that the coffee house is open. I don't even have to go out in search of them; they come here and find me, but in a more laid-back atmosphere than my job back east. Fortunately my work doesn't interfere with my social life. Basically, I keep the place stocked with coffee and pastries, and supervise the two waitresses I talked Mr. Conklin into hiring. This leaves plenty of time to hang out, while the boys are in school or asleep, and explore my new world.

And Carla, I feel freer from Paul each day. He's fading into the distant past, where he belongs. Although, sometimes I dream about him—long drawn out dreams of the two of us, face to face again, arguing endlessly. "Listen to me! Why won't you listen to what I have to say?" I scream this over and over again. Then, I wake up, and I'm crying.

My new friend, Harmony's guru, said that love is as hard to kick as heroin. I think that means the dreams are withdrawal symptoms and will pass when the addiction is broken.

The boys are fine. They're excited about living here and already know most of the Haight Street merchants, plus a few of our neighbors. They're in school now, making new friends and learning to be city kids. I'm relieved because at first, they had their reservations. For instance, when I asked how they liked it here after the first week had passed, Brad said, "There's a lot of dog shit in this town." And Doug told him, "When you learn not to step in dog shit, you become a city person."

I haven't stepped in dog shit for a week now, so it's all coming together, I'm sure.

That's the news for now. I'm going to a party tonight, my first social event in San Francisco. One of my waitresses will hang with the kids. But first I need to feed them, take a shower, and get gorgeous, all in the next hour, before this very cool guy arrives to pick me up. He's an Aquarian, a free spirit, a seeker of truth, a student of astrology, and an aspiring palm reader. He did a reading for me in the café last week and said my journey of self-discovery had only just begun. I hope the party is wild.

I miss you. I miss you. Give my love to Ray and the boys. Brad and Doug send love. They said to tell you they're looking forward to our first Christmas season without snow. I'm sending you photos. Please send us some too. Write soon.

Love,

Dorothy

PS: —I'm reading the Don Juan books, and I've tried grass. Both are wonderful. I've signed up for a seminar called *Thinking Magically*, presented by a psychic woman from Seattle. It's about learning to be a warrior in the world and pursuing my goals with unbending intention, to create the life I want to live. I can hardly wait.

Perfect Stranger Encounter #2

Steve

"No doubt about it, babe, you look good enough to eat," Steve said when he arrived to escort me to the party. He wore beige corduroy bellbottoms, a multi-colored polyester shirt, and a brown fringed vest. He flashed me a dimpled grin, and I melted. I'm a pushover for dimples.

"Well, let's hope so." I purred, gazing into his eyes. They were intensely blue, like Aquarian actor Paul Newman's, but something about them reminded me of my ex-husband's brown ones. "Your eyes have a faraway look," I said, "as though you're seeing me through a veil, or a rainbow—or like you suddenly landed here on Earth and are looking around, wondering what planet you're on."

Back in upstate New York, this verbal repartee would have been called nuts, but not in San Francisco. Steve was delighted by my observations. "How perceptive you are," he said, as the kids closed in to inspect Mom's new boyfriend. "You see, the truth is

65

that I live on a rainbow and come down to Earth every now and then to check things out. Problem is from down here you can't see the end of the rainbow, so I never stay long."

"Clever fellow," I said, admiring the width of his shoulders and his long wavy hair.

Brad and Doug exchanged looks and rolled their eyes.

"Another kook," Doug whispered.

"She's going through a stage," Brad explained, putting an arm around his brother. "Come on, let's go watch TV."

The party was everything I'd hoped it would be. It sprawled through seven rooms of a Victorian flat, near Oak and Ashbury, with bay windows, built-in bookcases, and fine old hardwood floors. In the front room, three longhaired men in drawstring pants were hunched over two guitars and a piano, playing their hearts out. The smell of incense, combined with the sharp smell of cigarette smoke and the sweet, pungent odor of pot, hung in the air.

Throughout the flat, people were dressed in bright, richly textured fabrics, and wore jingling bells, and Earth Shoes, and had neat names like Sky, or Morning Glory, or Fortune. A number of them were stoned out of their minds and "doing their thing."

In the dining room, a generously built woman, wearing two rings in her nose and one in an eyebrow, belly danced with abandon. In the sunroom off the kitchen, a spiritual type in a purple robe was up, up and away, in a perfect Lotus position. On the patio, an androgynous individual in skintight leather and an enormous Afro was heavily engaged in the seduction of a very slim, very young man.

The whole scene delighted me.

"This is Allison, Good Witch of the West and an all-around great lay," Steve said, presenting our hostess. Allison, slim, elegant, and self-confident, with the posture of a ballerina, was an "Auntie Mame" type in her early forties, dressed in flowing purple silk.

"He only says that because of those *nasty* rumors going around," she said, hugging him. "Not to mention my phone number scrawled on all those men's room walls."

They each smiled, and she winked at me. I got the feeling that her sexual appetite was a familiar joke between them.

"It's a pleasure to meet you, Dorothy. Explore, play; enjoy the party. Maybe later we'll get better acquainted." She kissed my cheek and my date's lips and floated away.

"Cool lady," I said. "Is she a good friend of yours?"

"She's my wife," Steve said, casually. "We have an open relationship."

Oh. Funny that Steve, who was an Aquarian, like Paul, should have an open marriage. Maybe it *is* more evolved, I thought—but surely all parties involved need to agree.

"I've been divorced two years." I heard someone say. "I'm trying to find myself."

"Who isn't?" I asked, of no one in particular, and Steve and I moved farther into the party.

What a far-out party that was! I learned a fabulous recipe for carrot cake. The secret is just the right measure of clover honey and organically grown carrots, of course. I was told good fortune was coming my way—but beware of the Queen of Cups. This information came from a dark, brooding, Tarot Card reader named Moses, who was originally from Cleveland. I listened in on major portions of the traumatic life story of a sweet, young, gay man fresh from the closet of his southern military family. Tennessee Williams lives!

"Dorothy! So glad you're here tonight." I turned toward the familiar, exuberant voice. Harmony, my new friend and Haight Street neighbor was in a form-fitting, fringed, canary-yellow dress with a leather peace sign at her throat, hugged me hello.

"*God,* you're a sexy bitch," she said, eyeing my form-fitting jeans, black boots, and low-cut purple sweater. "Having a good party, love?"

"I am."

"Where's Steve?"

"In there." I indicated the living room. "He said

he needed to talk to a man about some grass. I was just going to find him."

"Are you going to ball him?" Harmony's tone was casual—like she was inquiring what brand of dish soap I used.

"Yes, I think so."

"Well, you're in for a treat, then. He really knows his way around a woman."

"Know that for sure do you?" I was grinning.

"Would I kid a friend about something that important? That model's been road-tested, and sweetie, the motor purrs."

I found him in the sunroom, smoking a joint and listening to guitar music. "Hey there," I said. "It's getting late in the evening. Shall we go somewhere more private?"

Steve grinned and took my hand. "I was supposed to say that."

"So say it. Invite me to see your etchings."

"As it happens, I have no etchings to show, but I do have a private pad in the attic that's worth investigating."

The private pad upstairs was charming: old oak furniture, Indian bedspread, lots of plants, and a pleasing scent of sandalwood in the air. I was a bit uneasy about the party going on downstairs and us, alone together, upstairs, but didn't want to show it. I looked around, inspecting the room like I was thinking about renting it—until I turned around and there he was.

I drew my breath in sharply when his fingers found the stiffness of my nipples beneath my sweater and sighed deeply when he pinched and twisted them between his thumbs and forefingers. His eyes were open as he bent to kiss me. I gazed up into them. They are like Paul's eyes, I thought, veiled and far away. They leave me lonely.

I pushed the thought away. It was time to remove our clothes.

"You like him?" Steve asked. I smiled appreciatively at his cock, as I reached out to stroke it, making a mental note of its size, shape, and circumference.

"He's most impressive. Here, let me get a better look."

I bent to kiss it. It was smooth and hot, smelling faintly of soap and male arousal. I moved my tongue over it first, lapping at it, before working it carefully into my mouth. That was plenty of cock I was playing with. At first, I thought I might gag, but then I relaxed and, voilà, the whole thing was in to the hilt

Steve moaned. This impressed him, I could tell. Inspired by his response, I kept at it, sucking and flicking my tongue around the hot, smooth skin of his shaft until he moaned steadily and my jaw muscles began to ache. Whoever said the way to a man's heart is through his stomach didn't know a lot about sucking cock.

"How did you learn to give such great head?"

"I practice, diligently," I replied, straight-faced, "and have a genuine love for the sport."

"Your turn," he said later, as his tongue teased my swollen labia, seeking out and easily finding my hard little clit. I sighed happily as he lapped and sucked, working it with great expertise until I gasped and moaned with pleasure as my orgasm built and broke over me like a wave.

Later, we smoked and talked and drank organic grape juice, cuddled on his bed like old friends. No worries if he'd still love me tomorrow, I felt good with him right now.

"Far out, hot lady," he said, kissing me. "You really come when you come."

I smiled happily, because I actually *had* come for a change, and my heart, mind, and satisfied body were one and at peace. A stray thought of Paul came to mind, but I pushed it aside. It had no place in what was happening.

Let's hear it for California! I wanted to shout. There's mellow, man, mellow, and being laid back, and finding yourself, and carrot cake, and smoking joints before having sex. But best of all, there are orgasms out here on the West Coast. Dorothy, welcome home!

Perfect Strangers

CHAPTER FIVE

The weeks passed, and the spinning wheel turned. Every day I felt more certain that somehow, my wish had been granted and I'd become seventeen again. I felt like the proverbial kid in the candy store we keep hearing about. I couldn't get enough of that sweet stuff.

And it beat marriage by a long shot, as far as I was concerned. To me, marriage meant always having to say, "I'm sorry." While now, I was being wined, dined, admired, and pursued; playing it cool, and apologizing for nothing. Way more fun if you ask me. And it was so easy to be with a stranger. Easy to set aside my fears and insecurities and just be myself— whoever I was.

I had nothing to lose after all—it didn't matter if a stranger didn't like me.

"Jeremy is a witch," Harmony confided before introducing us. "He's *terribly* Scorpio. You'll *love* the experience."

While I didn't exactly love the experience, I *was* out searching for the new and unusual. A witch with flowing hair and a spooky brass medallion sounded like just the thing, although his look was a bit intimidating.

Still, he assured me he was a white witch and entertained me with tales of spells he had known and loved.

Getting into the spirit of the occasion I went to bed with him, hoping he'd magic up a few orgasms for me. No such luck. He may have been a witch, but he was no mind reader. I lay there afterward aroused, but unsatisfied, still smiling with the allure of a siren, and frustrated enough to scream. Somewhere inside my head, Paul was right there with me, sneering. *So this one didn't satisfy you either, Dorothy? I wonder what's wrong with* him.

Drop dead, I thought, but insecurity gnawed at me. *Was* there something wrong with me? I didn't know but planned to keep researching until I found out.

My next lover, Kyle, was a fast-talking real-estate broker, who claimed that his deepest wish was one good woman to love, but never found one he was willing to commit to. In bed, he executed an intricate lovemaking style, worthy of Penthouse Forum, but clearly not tailored to me. I lay beneath him thinking— why, why, why, aren't I home doing something interesting, like helping the kids with their homework? Excellent question, I thought, once I was out from under and on my way home. I'll have to give that some thought.

Because I put my attention on cocks, cocks became attentive to me. Gradually, I developed such a rapport with them that when I felt turned on to a man, his cock would present itself in my mind, and I'd know what it looked like before he undressed—another latent talent coming to the surface. If only there was a way to turn this clever parlor trick into a marketable skill. I could give lectures, I thought, visualizing myself in a seductive gown, standing before a penis shaped podium. The audience was a sea of women's faces.

"Sisters," I begin, "you are here to learn to develop your skill in visualizing the cock size of a fully dressed man. I have made a lifelong study of this subject, which has called for years of hard work and tireless dedication. I like to think of it as a private study of private parts."

Meanwhile, back at the coffeehouse, I was having a great time performing a fairly intricate juggling act with a growing number of boyfriends. A few of them were prone to dropping into the coffeehouse while the boys were at school, to find out if I'd be free later in the evening. If more than one of them were to get the same idea at the same time, things could get confusing.

Fortunately, I had an excellent rapport with both waitresses, who watched my social life get underway with amazement and unrestrained curiosity. Anne, a naïve, twenty-three-year-old from the mid-west, somehow interpreted what I was doing as romantic and wanted to help. Diane, who'd been seeing the same guy since high school and never experienced an orgasm of any kind, cheered me on. "I wish I had the guts to do what you're doing," she said. Between the two of them, they helped me handle the situation and keep everyone separated.

Initially, I tried to keep my sex life a secret from my sons, not wishing to damage their little psyches by letting them know their mother played around. To this end, I made certain that if a man was in my bed at night, he'd be gone before morning.

This worked well until the Friday night when Bobby, a fellow Haight St. merchant, came by for dinner and stayed late into the evening to have sex with me after the boys were asleep. Somehow I slipped up, and we both fell asleep afterward. I woke to the sound of Saturday morning cartoons.

"Oh God," I wailed, poking him awake. "What am I going to do?"

"I'll jump out the window," he offered, pulling on his clothes. "Where are my shoes?"

"Oh my god, they're in the living room with the kids!" I was close to panic when I heard a polite knock at the door."

"Hey, Mom..."

"What is it, Brad? Is something the matter? Wait, darling, I'm not up yet."

Good grief, what do I do now? He's going to come in, and be traumatized, and tell terrible stories about me to his analyst when he's thirty-five.

"Nothing's wrong, Mom. I just wanted to tell you, Bobby left his shoes in the living room near the couch. Hi, Bobby," he called through the door.

Yes, I decided, the boys are grown up enough to

understand that their mother is a sexual being, and initiated a talk on this subject the next day during dinner.

"So," I began, clearing my throat and spearing a French fry with my fork, "as you may have noticed, well… now that I'm single, I have some men friends."

"We noticed," Brad said. He took a large bite of his burger, smirking and chewing at the same time.

"Do you sleep with all of them?" Doug wanted to know.

"Well no, not all of them," I said, which was sort of true, "but some of them."

"How come you do it?" Doug asked, looking up at me.

I smiled at the question and brushed his soft brown hair back from his eyes while my mind darted around deciding how to answer. "Well…" I said, "I do it because I'm a grown woman and enjoy male company," The kids were silent a minute, kicking that one around in their heads.

"Are you going to marry one of those guys?" Brad asked after a while.

"I…I…don't know." I felt confused to the point of stammering because my son asked me a simple question. "I thought I would, Brad…when your dad and I were first divorced, but now I'm not sure. I think for a while, I want it to be just us three, and in my private time to enjoy myself as an adult. Can you understand that?"

"Hey, Mom, you don't have to explain yourself to us," Brad said.

"Yeah," Doug added, "We understand you just want to sleep with them. It's OK. You used to be sad a lot when you and Dad were married. You laugh a lot now. We like seeing you have a good time."

"Just don't do anything dumb, like marry someone before *we* say he's cool enough," Brad said, as he and Doug finished their meal and went off to do their homework.

Perfect Stranger Encounter #3

Light Angel

I met Victor at Harmony's Summer Solstice party in the Castro. I felt unusually free that night with the boys gone camping in Big Sur with Steve and Allison, and thought if I met someone appealing I'd take him home with me.

Victor was slim and fair-skinned, with thinning blond hair and looked to be about my age, which was thirty-two that summer. He wore a white T-shirt, black yoga pants, and Birkenstocks. The top of my head came to his shoulder making him about five nine. His pale, slightly bulbous blue eyes had the soft, gentle look of a dreamer. Pisces, I decided. No doubt.

He approached me at the buffet table as I was sampling smoked oysters. I caught his admiring look and it pleased me. I knew I looked good that night in a tank-top as green as my eyes and jeans that fit like a second skin.

"You have beautiful light," he said. "Pure and shining. I saw it right away."

Although I claimed to choose my men with care and deliberation—the truth was I decided to have sex with Victor five minutes after meeting him because he told me I had beautiful light.

It wasn't unusual for someone to say that in California in 1976. Everyone was into some aspect of extrasensory perception back then. I figured the guy could see auras—more power to him—and took it as a step up on the evolutionary ladder from being told I looked hot. In fact, I was so pleased by his spiritual approach, I hustled him right home to learn, firsthand, how a man of higher consciousness goes down on a woman.

"Such an evolved vibration," he said, teasing my nipples. "Lie back. Let me pleasure you." We sat, side by side, on my purple tie-dyed bedspread in my plant-filled bedroom. Smoke from a lighted stick of incense curled toward the ceiling filling the room with the scent of jasmine. *Like a Bridge over Troubled Water*, crooned Simon and Garfunkel from the stereo and I lay back, my mind considerably eased when Victor went down on me.

No problem finding my clit for this guy, or slipping a knowing finger into each of my openings, driving me wild. Like other Pisces lovers I've known, he was highly skilled at going down on a woman. I almost passed out from pleasure when he did some odd little trick with his lip muscles, while, so help me, he hummed.

I grinned at the sight of his cock—which was *exactly* as I pictured it, not long, maybe five inches, but nice and thick. Stroking it, I measured it against my hand to be sure. I was right-on. Just another talent, I thought, like playing the flute or excelling in acrobatics—with enough practice a skill develops, and there you are.

His cock was rock-hard when I went down on him; hot, smooth, and fragrant with arousal. Droplets of pre-come seeped from the tiny mouth-like opening at its tip. I licked them lightly with my tongue, then deep-throated him, showing off my skills. My firm little breasts and hardened nipples pressed up against his balls, sending little electric jolts of pleasure through me, making me squirm.

Climbing astride him, I squeezed down on his cock with my vaginal muscles, grinding my clit against the base of it, slowly first, then building momentum. My breasts caressed his chest when I bent to kiss him. His arms encircled me and his leg hitched over my hip. Still coupled, without breaking rhythm; he flipped us over to continue our dance. We finished long after midnight and lay spooning, contentedly, his arms around me, cock half-hard, still inside.

"Shall I stay?" he asked," and I turned to him in the darkness thinking how odd it was that sleeping with a man seemed so much more intimate than having sex with him.

"Yes," I said, surprising myself. "Stay."

It felt good to fall asleep in someone's arms. Good to wake and find him beside me the next morning—better still after early morning sex. We agreed he'd stay until the day the kids returned and after informing Mr. Conklin, Anne, and Diane that I had a virus, I settled down with Victor to do some serious shacking up.

That afternoon, we held hands and walked in the sand along the vastness of Ocean Beach watching the waves roll in and out. Later we sipped chardonnay and nibbled appetizers, in the wood-paneled Cliff House Bar, while looking out at the sun setting over the sea. The next day we explored Marin County in Victor's ancient VW bus. I lay on a blanket he'd brought along staring up at the giant Redwood trees in Muir Woods, while his knowing lips and tongue sucked and nibbled at my labia, teasing my clit until I climaxed, screaming my pleasure to the sky.

I was starting to like the man, whoever he was. As our mini-lifetime together progressed, I learned more about him. He was an English professor from Boston, who'd married his childhood sweetheart, with whom he thought he'd had a stormy but successful marriage. He discovered he was mistaken when his wife filed for divorce and left him for another woman. Devastated, he emptied his bank account and took off on the bus, leaving everything he thought he cared about behind, while he roamed the country, seeking clarity. He arrived in the sexual Mecca of San Francisco, met me, and there we were.

The problem with Victor began on our fourth day together, when I learned still another of life's little lessons: things are not always as they seem. By then we were so comfortable with each other, my lover was inspired to open up and reveal his true self to me. Unfortunately, that was the problem.

So, there I was in my filmy dressing gown, curled up with Victor on my rose-patterned sofa, gazing out my front window at a star-filled night, reflecting on the nature of relationships—why they work, why they don't—when I realized he'd just informed me he wasn't an ordinary human being. In fact, and trust me, I could have lived happily never knowing this—*he wasn't a human being at all.* He was a Light Angel of the Lord.

"Not...a human being?" I spoke slowly, regretfully, suspecting this new information was going to interfere with some powerful orgasms. "I...ah...wish you'd mentioned this earlier."

"It's not something I bring up right away. But it's time for you to know."

Know what? Why tell me? I wanted a fling while my kids were away. Nothing complicated...Please.

"I follow the light, Dorothy, and guide those with a clear light home to my father."

"Your father...?" My voice had a quiver in it I couldn't seem to control. "Like *God* you mean?"

Victor nodded. "Yes," he said, and eyes sparkling, he explained about the lights he saw, which weren't exactly auras, but rather, brightly colored blobs that burst from individual energy fields and went *whoosh* up into the ether.

I stared at him, remembering he'd said his ex-wife tried to murder him by lacing his orange juice with sixty hits of acid. *Dear God, since your name has been brought into this, please tell me—how much of that juice did he drink?*

Turns out, Victor became aware he was an angel quite soon after drinking the spiked juice. "It was then," he said serenely, "I realized the true nature of who I was."

"Are you saying you're some kind of minister?" I asked, grasping at straws.

"I'm saying who I am, Dorothy." He shrugged and flashed a confident smile. "I appear to be a man. I'll even bleed if you cut me. But the truth is, I'm an angel. Some people become hostile when they learn the truth, but my father watches over me. I can't be harmed. Isn't that so Father?"

He was speaking directly to God now, who, judging by Victor's glassy stare, was hanging out somewhere over my left shoulder.

"Jesus Christ," I whispered.

"My brother," Victor said and smiled again.

My heart was racing so fast I could hardly breathe. The harsh reality was intruding into my fantasy world—leaving me alone and vulnerable with a man lost in his. He needs to leave, I thought, before I annoy him in some way and he decides I'm anti-Light Angel. After all, his father could get pissed.

Victor took my hand, "Ready for bed?"

"I...well...I have this headache."

"I was thinking of sleeping," he said, kindly. "It's very late."

I was afraid to ask him to leave because there was a look in his eyes I couldn't define, except that it scared me. The man had a delusion, a fixed idea he believed in—he might be angry if I threatened it, murder me even, and my sons would return home tomorrow evening to discover my decomposing body and be traumatized for life. Maybe, I thought, climbing reluctantly into bed, that's why there's so much murder and mayhem in the world today—people threaten other people's delusions, and they don't like it.

He fell asleep quickly, after commenting on some particularly bright light pouring from me. *Whooosh!* Up into the ether and away.

Too frightened to move, I lay awake beside him for the remainder of the night mulling it all over in my head. So many ways to roll with the punches, I decided. We all choose one way or another.

The sun was out the next morning, and I felt brave again. After coffee, I told Victor, honestly enough, that I, a mere human being, felt undeserving of a Light Angel of the Lord—and since my boys would be returning home in the evening, he needed to leave. To my relief, he seemed to understand and offered no arguments. He kissed me before leaving and told me again I had beautiful light. Then he was gone like he'd never existed.

I double-locked the door behind him, took a long, deep breath, and exhaled sharply. Exhausted, I made my way to the bedroom and crawled back into bed. I slept all day, waking shortly before the kids arrived home.

"Mom!" Doug's voice filled the room, and he flung himself onto the sofa beside me. "We had a great time! We swam and hiked, and I got to ride a horse. Brad beat me up two times, *for no reason,* and once he made my nose bleed."

"Cool trip," Brad said. "I wish you could have come with us. What did you do while we were gone?"

"Oh, I kind of took it easy for a few days, lay around. I had company part of the time."

"Did you get lonely without us?" Doug asked, cuddling closer. His dear little body felt warm and comforting in my arms.

I nodded. "I missed you like crazy. I'm so glad you're back."

I hung out with the kids for the next week or so and brooded about men and the unfairness of life in general.

"The strangers get stranger and stranger," I complained in a letter to Carla. "And although I realize that a man I can have orgasms with is not to be cast away lightly, I see no chance of a future for me and a Light Angel of the Lord."

So it was back to the drawing board for me as I continued my search for sexual self-discovery. Like that guy in the beer commercial, I wanted all the gusto I could get. But, more often than not, I was tormented by a persistent, nagging sense of failure—as I lay in a frustrated tangle of nerve endings, under some hunk who was basking in his own afterglow.

Why, why, why, don't I have vaginal orgasms? I agonized—while in my mind, Paul sneered at me, as he waltzed with Cassandra, through a life that was one big long come.

Perfect Strangers

Perfect Stranger Encounter # 4

Jake

I was on my hands and knees the first time I met Jake, which, considering the relationship that ensued was clearly a symbolic beginning. It was closing time, and the coffeehouse was empty. I was alone in front of the counter sponging up a spill when I felt someone watching me. At my eye level, I was face to face with a man's crotch.

Well hello, sweetheart, I thought and gazed up into a pair of piercing, dark eyes that bore into me with unrestrained curiosity.

The scene turned me on. I fantasized the stranger approaching me, silently unzipping his fly, and thrusting his sizable erection into my mouth. "Take it," he said, and my lips parted. My long dark curls cascaded down my back as my face tilted up to him, sucking, licking, breathing him in, my eyes closed in ecstasy.

The man observed me, patiently. Somehow, I knew he was sharing my fantasy. We held our positions, eyes locked, for what seemed like a long time. Finally, I came to my senses and got to my feet.

"Hello, sweetheart." The man's greeting echoed my thought. "Who are you?"

"I'm Dorothy," I said, breathing a little hard.

"Jake." His voice was calm and soothing. He stood still, allowing me to study him.

My mom, back in New York, would have found him crude and low class—like Stanley Kowalski in *Streetcar Named Desire*—the kind of man who undressed women with his eyes and treated them like sexual objects. I'd been taught to avoid men like that.

Jake looked to be about thirty, big-boned, with high cheekbones, a strong chin, and full sensual lips. He wore a white shirt open at the throat, with a black leather jacket, and a military-style cap with an insignia on it. He had the look of a sailor, or a pirate, even, minus the scar on his cheek and black patch over one eye. It turned out he was a former Merchant Marine, also from the east coast, and co-owned the used furniture and antique shop down the street.

He explained that he was a double Scorpio, the zodiac sign that ruled sexuality and consequently, had a super-sexual viewpoint on life.

"I'm a great lover of women," he continued. "Penetrating the mystery of a woman is my greatest joy, and each one is a separate mystery. My deepest desire is to know and please them all. Any color, any age. I love making women feel good."

This predilection led to the breakup of his stormy five-year marriage to a stripper from Florida, whom he claimed to still love. "She wanted me all to herself," he said, throwing up his hands in a universal, 'what else can I say' gesture.

I couldn't tell if he was serious or feeding me a line, but something about him reached out to me. Some promise of dark mystery and unrestrained passion, and a simple, lustful approach to life—not to mention the almost overpowering aura of sexuality that emanated from his deep-set hooded eyes. They quickly penetrated my outer armor and got right down to checking out my inner core.

The café had emptied by seven-thirty. The waitresses had gone home, and the kids were staying overnight with school friends. Jake sat at a table watching me close down for the night.

"Dorothy, I know this will sound like a corny old pickup line," he said with disarming earnestness, "but you are so beautiful that when I saw you, my heart raced so fast, I couldn't catch my breath. Let me take you to dinner and we'll get better acquainted."

What balls this guy's got, I thought, with admiration. *Hands me a corny old pickup line; tells me he knows it's a corny old pickup line—and guess what, it's going to work.*

"Well, all right!" I said, grinning broadly and gazing into his eyes. "Only a fool would turn down a man with a sexual viewpoint on life."

"Dinner with you was a pleasure, " Jake said, as we left Little Joe's in North Beach and stepped out into the bustle of Broadway on a Saturday night. "I learn a lot about a woman by watching her eat."

"And what secrets did I reveal to you by the way I ate my lasagna?" I was teasing, but he took it straight. I tried to remember if Scorpios had a sense of humor.

"A woman who's passionate about food, and who savors the taste, and smell, and texture of it in her mouth," he explained, "will be that same way in bed."

"Then I trust you observed my hearty appetite?"

Jake grinned. "There's not much about a woman I miss," he said, and I sensed he wasn't bragging, but simply stating a fact. He turned to me, his eyes gleaming with excitement.

"Dorothy, have you ever wandered around Broadway in the evening? No? Fantastic! Let me show it to you. We can check out the strip joints and the peep shows. There's a full moon tonight. People will be feeling wild. Broadway is sleazy." His words conveyed no criticism; he simply told me how it was.

"*Sleazy.*" I repeated the word, exploring the sound of it. I smiled into his eyes. "Okay, sweetheart," I said, "show me what sleazy looks like."

Jake was like a sailor on shore leave; brash, bold, ready for action—like Broadway itself, raw and angry with sex. It was his element and I moved into it with him, seeing it through his eyes. Broadway *was* sleazy, no arguments there—but for me that night, it was magic, pure and simple.

It was a warm winter night with dark clouds gathering, and the thick, moist air felt like rain was on the way. We strolled, arm in arm, witnessing men and women all around us, men and men, too, sizing one another up with hot eyes, waving their sexuality before them like flags; their desire vibrating in the night air.

We peeked into the smoky depths of San Francisco's original gentlemen's establishment, the Condor Club. There, I gawked at Carol Doda, Broadway's first topless dancer and at her artificially enhanced, size forty-four breasts. They stood straight up while she lay flat—like two living monuments to the discovery of silicone. Back out on Broadway, barkers called out to us, enticing us into similar, dimly lit clubs to witness "genuine acts of love." Name your preference, they promised, your perversion, your personal proclivity; see it performed live inside for your pleasure.

We perused a "dirty" bookstore, the likes of which I'd not seen before, with its non-descript proprietor and furtive, all male clientele—while sharp little rushes of excitement I wouldn't admit to, shot their way between my thighs—as I gawked, hardly believing, at images from my own secret fantasies.

"Does that turn you on?" Jake indicated an image of an orgy on a magazine cover, inquiring casually, as though the question wouldn't make me blush.

"Ohhh..." I breathed softly. "I didn't know people really did that."

He smiled, smug with knowing, and I thought, this man knows my fantasies. But how can he know? Is he some sort of psychic—or do my fantasies simply show? I wondered as we stood pressed together in dark little booths at the peep shows that smelled like half of humanity had been in them before us.

"So there I was," I later wrote Carla, "cramming quarters into the film machine in this slimy peep show booth. What was that like for me, you ask; well educated, well brought up lady that I am? Well, for openers, I was speechless with embarrassment—but my insides were clenched with excitement, my nipples hard at attention, and if you want the truth, my pants were wet.

I wonder what *Paul* would think about that!

A fine rain began falling as we left Broadway around midnight, after stopping in at a jazz club. We barely made it to Jake's truck without getting wet. I said little during the ride back to Haight Street. I was so aroused I could hardly sit still. The air in the cab of the truck crackled with excitement and the rain pelted down.

"You were right," I said later, back in my apartment. "Broadway *is* sleazy."

"And you loved it, right?" he asked, like he knew it was so and laughed.

I blushed. "Not *loved*, exactly… Found *interesting* maybe… And well, yes… I *loved* it."

Jake sat on the padded armchair in my bedroom, watching me. I stood near the window looking out at the rain and saw him reflected in the glass. Attempting to mask my sudden shyness, I fiddled with the stereo, while the man waited with his eyes hot on me, watching my every move.

He's not real, I thought, *I made him up in a fantasy, and now he's arrived to act it out.*

Ten feet away, Jake didn't move a muscle, but I felt like he'd come closer—and the part of me that didn't stiffen like a wary cat, welcomed him with open arms.

"Come here, sweetheart," he said. "Let me make you feel good."

Jake stared intently into my eyes, willing me into his fantasy. Rising from his chair, he scooped me up in his arms and carried me to the bed. Slowly, without breaking eye contact, he pulled my T-shirt up over my head, undressing me to the waist.

"A perfect handful, I knew they'd be," he said, cupping my bared breasts in work-hardened hands. I drew my breath in sharply when he pinched my stiffened nipples between his thumbs and forefingers. "Lie back," he said, smiling. "Let's see what the rest of you looks like."

Unzipping my jeans, he eased them down over my hips and legs. When I was naked, he pressed me back against the pillows, gazing at me for a long moment before proceeding to explore my body like it was uncharted territory.

"You're such a beautiful woman," he murmured, and firmly, with some underlying hint of roughness, parted my legs. Half smiling, he spat a glob of saliva onto his fingers and rubbed it deliberately over my swollen sex. Without any sense of haste, he stroked, teased, and delighted, sending hot jolts of arousal coursing through me. Jake slipped thick fingers inside me, moving them around, twisting, massaging, thrusting, and all the while attuning his attention to where my excitement lay.

"Tell me what you want," he whispered hoarsely. "I'm your seductor, but I'm also your slave. I'll do *anything* to please you."

"There," I whispered, gasping for breath, "Like that. Right there. Don't stop!"

Jake found his mark. His knowing fingers and hot wet mouth pinched, licked, and sucked my clit. I moaned steadily, hands in his hair, back arching as he parted my asscheeks and inserted a finger and pushed me straight over the edge. Screaming, I exploded into a thousand tiny fragments of pleasured flesh.

When I opened my eyes, I saw he was watching me. There was no particular expression on his face, just a broad gleam of triumph in his eyes.

That wasn't hard now was it Just give in. Go with the pleasure.

He directed me to my knees for the next act of the fantasy.

"Suck my cock, woman," he ordered, and I did so, my mouth filled with his hardness and salty taste, and I breathed in his heady aroma. I accepted him obediently, as I did in my fantasy, licking at his cock-head, lapping at it, teasing it with the warm wetness of my lips. I made him moan with pleasure by swiping his shaft with my tongue as I deep-throated him. My hands cupped his balls, which tightened with excitement, and my body responded with a non-stop, electric tingling between my thighs.

Jaws aching, I sucked for all I was worth—until he'd had enough.

Finally, heavily, he mounted me, plunging in with a moan of ecstasy, abandoning himself to pleasure with the ease of an animal. Thrusting, grinding, probing, he claimed me as his woman, seeking my excitement with his own.

"Yes!" I cried out, "Yes!" And moaning, I raised my hips to meet his thrusts, while his hands held mine above my head and pinned them to the mattress. Writhing beneath him, my breath came in gasps, and my excitement rose like mercury in a thermometer, as I groped for the unfamiliar wavelength of out-of-control.

Finally, his eyes glazed over with passion. "Oh my cock, my nuts!" he moaned, humping like a crazed animal. "I'm going to come now. Take my come woman. Take it!"

We were drenched with sweat by the time we finished and lay resting, while our heart rates slowed and our breathing returned to normal. I was half asleep, pressed up against Jake, with my head on his shoulder and his hand on my thigh. It was still raining. I could hear the drops spatter against the window. It felt warm and safe inside.

"You came when I went down on you, but not with my cock in your cunt," he said. "Am I right?"

"There really isn't much about a woman you miss," I said. "Yes, I came earlier when you went down on me, but not with your cock inside. I came close but didn't quite get there. I only come from oral sex or manually, or with a vibrator. I've never had a vaginal orgasm in my life."

"Oh yeah? Well, some women can, some can't," Jake said, casually, as though I hadn't just confessed my deepest, darkest secret. "My wife was like that. She'd get close when we fucked, but couldn't climax no matter what we did. It drove her nuts."

"Yes." I said, "I understand. So, what happened?"

"Well, she finally relaxed and let go one day— but let me tell you, I worked my balls off on it for a long-ass time. I tried *everything* with that woman. We did it front-ways, sideways, doggie style; even upside down." Jake grinned. "So, what about you, Dorothy— what turns you on the most?"

"Besides oral sex, you mean? Good question," I said, regarding him with affection. "No one ever asked me that before. Do you have…um…any suggestions?"

Jake's look was penetrating. "I could come up with an idea or two—if you want me to."

If I wanted him to?

"I want you to," I said envisioning the many hot nights to come, and the fantasies in my head just waiting to be orchestrated. Again, I caught the gleam of triumph in his eyes.

He nodded with satisfaction. "Dorothy, I know a hot woman when I see one, and *you*, my dear, are a hot woman. No worries. We'll experiment and figure out what turns you on."

And so, a working relationship was born. There was Jake—tireless, dedicated, available day or night, for a woman in need of his particular talents. And me, a sexually frustrated woman determined to end my sexual limitations. From that evening on we became two minds with but a single thought, each dedicated to the all-important discovery of what makes Dorothy come?

Dear Carla,

Sorry for the long silence. My mom just returned home after flying in for a two-week visit. The boys loved having her. She took them clothes shopping and cooked all their favorite foods. I showed her around the Haight Ashbury, which she found outlandish. It made me sad that she takes prescription tranquilizers, daily—but was shocked to learn I'd tried grass.

Anyway, I've stored up information to share, but this business of being a single parent takes lots of time. In the last month, for example, I've made two trips to the Haight-Ashbury Free Clinic (Doug for stitches, Brad for allergy shots), two trips to the dentist (Doug for a cleaning, Brad to fix a tooth he chipped playing football), and back to the clinic (Doug again for a sore throat). And then there's food shopping, a never-ending task with two growing boys, as well as shopping for provisions to keep the coffee shop going.

But then, there's my free time. To do a thing well you've got to work at it, so, since casual sex is the name of the game—I'm working on being the best damn player in town. Today, I've taken the phone off the hook and chained my left leg to my desk. I'll be rescued in a few hours when the boys come home from school. In the meantime here's my news.

First of all, a riddle: what's the best thing that could happen to a sex-crazed, frustrated woman of the seventies, wandering through the male population in search of the perfect, and by this I mean vaginal, orgasm? Give up? Okay, here's the answer..

She could get lucky and meet a sex-crazed, double Scorpio—a friendly, "stoned age" child of the seventies—whose life is a never-ending sexual fantasy. Far out, don't you think? His name is Jake, and I'm having the time of my life with his brand of fine madness—although I'm not rushing to the phone to tell my mom all about him.

You see, he's bright, but not educated. His grammar is marginal, and he's unarguably a bit on the uncouth side. A former Merchant Marine, he moved here from the East Coast a few years ago. He and his partner buy up old furniture and household items and sell the stuff in a small store they've leased on Haight St. His dream of a perfect life is to find a woman who'll love him enough to take him to the Caribbean Islands and support him in tropical luxury, while he does what he does best.

You can just stop shaking your head and muttering to yourself. In spite of everything this guy is something out of the ordinary—and you know how I respond to that. Carla, Jake has an unusual way of living. Somehow, he's escaped the tiny, electronic, sin detecting device we all have implanted behind our left ears when we're little. You know the one I mean. It says *"sin, sin, sin,"* in a grim little whisper, and makes us feel guilty so we do *right* instead of *wrong.*

Since Jake doesn't get the concept of sin, he ignores this nonsense entirely, believing devoutly in the *"if it feels good, do it,"* philosophy of life. It's a different point of view than the one I've been working with, and since all else has failed so far, I've decided to give it a go.

Once I'd confessed to him my deep, dark secret of high and dry nights, he seemed to feel I'd placed myself and my sexual frustrations into his capable hands. (This is, I'm sure, bringing great joy to the manipulative side of his Scorpio nature.) So, Jake, the puppet master is hard at work creating scenes custom designed to pull my strings—and help me determine what brings the most joy to this eager little body. To this end he pokes and pries into my mind, demanding to know what I'm *really* feeling at any given moment. Then, based on his findings he sets up situations designed to reveal my sexual inhibitions—and shades of *The Exorcist* drives them out!

Although other men come and go in my life, Jake remains constant. I don't love him, but he's hot, wild, and outlandish. We laugh a lot together. He's the chief honcho of all the strangers.

"I wanna be the only one," he says, his dark eyes gleaming, "who knows about the rest." And so he encourages me to share the smallest details of a night spent with another man.

In his way, he shares himself with me too. His record for non-stop sex—aside from food and bathroom breaks, you may care to know—was eighteen hours.

This happened when he was a seaman visiting a whore house in the Caribbean. He pleased the women to such a degree they refused to let him leave and held him as a willing captive until it was time for his ship to sail.

"Them bitches almost killed me," Jake smirked at the memory. "I was so sore I could barely walk, but it was worth every second." He claimed to know at age fifteen, while screwing a sixteen-year-old girl in a dingy Baltimore Maryland hallway that he was born to fuck.

Jake feels that although we put men on the moon and perform medical miracles, we're not a civilized society when women go to sleep at night hungry for orgasms. Oddly poetic, don't you think? Not everyone says this. I wish there were many more like him in this uptight world.

Since we see each other often now, I've introduced him to the kids. I was curious what they'd think of him, since, although I'd *never* admit it to them, their instincts about people appear to be better than mine. Outspoken little know-it-alls that they are, they let me know when they meet a guy who's not good enough to mess around with their mother. Like the time I was checking out this lawyer at the coffeehouse and Brad called me aside: "Don't you know that guy's a flake?" he asked, so earnestly, that I took a closer look and saw that the kid was right on.

The boys said they liked Jake—once I'd reassured them I was only playing and wasn't planning on moving him in or anything serious like that. They say he's crazy but cool, and agree with me that he's honest and real—which surely counts for something in this insane world. By the way, in case you're wondering, as my friend Harmony was: Jake, the super stud is a respectable size, but *not* hung like a horse. This surprised me when I first saw his cock, and I told him so. He said he was living proof to the world that the biggest wasn't always the best.

Enough said about Jake for now. The kids— when they're not up for repairs at the doctor or dentist—are doing fine. They've made new friends and are adjusting to the city and all its strange ways. Yesterday, I noticed Doug barely looked up from his book when a guy with a sizable snake wrapped around his neck went prancing by. I guess they're settling in.

My job is working out okay, as dead-end jobs go; not demanding, and a great place to win friends and influence people, if you know what I mean. The place is beginning to show a minuscule profit since I talked Mr. Conklin into easing off on the alleged art and expanding into food. He's so pleased about this he's given me an equally minuscule raise.

I'm using the extra money to decorate the apartment. Last week I put up new bamboo window blinds, and *Rolling Stones* posters in the boys' room, and one of Janis Joplin and another of Bob Dylan, in mine. I bought brightly colored Pakistani bedspreads for all three of us. I got a deal at Mother Fern, the plant shop across the street, and now my windows are crowded with pots of Spider Plants, Philodendrons, ferns, a Christmas cactus, and two Mother-in-law tongues. Jake, the ever helpful, has been turning up with solid oak dressers and nightstands, a desk, even a toaster—which cost me almost nothing. (I do love a man with more than one talent.) All in all, the place is beginning to look like home. And that's the news for tonight. Life is good after all. Miss you always. Please visit.

Love,
Dorothy

Perfect Strangers

CHAPTER SIX

Once I finally opened up and began telling my sexual secrets, I couldn't stop talking. This was fine with Jake; he wanted to hear it all. Night after night he'd appear at my door, materializing like some horny genie from wherever he'd spent his day.

After the boys were asleep, I lay in my candle-lit bedroom, naked and relaxed with Jake beside me on my bed. There, with a Joni Mitchell album playing softly in the background—I related episode after episode of my long, frustrating sexual history.

"My first time with Paul was a week after meeting him. We did it in my bedroom, less than a year after my dad passed away. What with me being barely seventeen and Paul so much older, I suppose the whole thing had Freudian overtones from the start."

"It happened while my mom was out of town visiting her sister. I was alone and unguarded for the first time in my life with a sophisticated older man. My poor mom was so upset when she learned her little girl wasn't pure anymore." I paused to take a breath, while Jake watched me intently, as though my sad little monologue was the most fascinating thing he'd ever heard.

"So that was your first time ever? You were a
107

virgin cunt. God, I'd have loved being the first one to take you." His eyes lit up at the thought.

"Yes, sweetheart," I said laughing, "a 'virgin cunt', as you so elegantly put it; thrilled at the prospect of becoming a woman, and thinking I'd found Prince Charming in the flesh. I thought he'd initiate me into the sacred rituals of lovemaking, and I'd see stars, and hear bells, and float away on a silver cloud of ecstasy like in a Hollywood film. But it didn't happen that way; didn't even come close." I turned my head and stared at the shadow of the candle flame on the wall near the bed. Remembering was getting me a little depressed.

"It happened quickly, like in a dream. First, we were kissing, which was wonderful. I felt buttery soft like I was melting inside, with my eyes closed and my head heavy and tilted back onto the softness of a pillow. When I opened them again, somehow, we were naked. I recall looking at his cock and thinking *good lord that thing's big*. It was the first time I'd seen one except for small boys and statues in museums. My parents took great care that I never saw my dad naked, and I hadn't realized an erect penis would be that large. Paul moved on top of me and began pushing it in. It hurt like mad. I wanted to push him off me and forget the whole thing, but at the same time I wanted to help him get it in because I wanted to see those stars."

I felt sad remembering that. Jake seemed to understand and held me closer, caressing my breasts possessively. It was almost a gesture of affection.

"I read in *Peyton Place*—the red-hot, tell-all novel by Grace Metalious, we girls read in secret when I was a teenager in the 50s—that the woman could help by raising her hips, so I did that, and he got it in. But I didn't see any stars that night, and he came very quickly. I recall thinking, I'm a woman now and feeling proud and excited about that, but at the same time some other part of me was saying, *'This is it?'* and feeling cheated. Then we both said 'I love you' and I thought that meant everything would be fine."

Jake studied my face while I told my story. His big hand stroked my body. "Did it get better later on?"

I sighed. "Yes and no. I loved sex but wasn't getting enough out of it no matter how hard I tried. Then I began feeling guilty. I was convinced Paul was an experienced lover since he'd lived with a woman in her thirties prior to meeting me, so I thought the problem must be mine. But once, maybe a year after we married, I lay on my stomach after we'd had sex and he played with my clit for a long time. And for once he found the exactly right spot—*and stayed on it*—moving his fingers in a slow circular motion. I was so relaxed I forgot to worry about whether I'd come or not, and focused instead on the lovely sensations that built and intensified until—surprise!—I had an orgasm that must have gone on for five minutes.

Jake sat up at attention. I was nearing a high point in my story as far as he was concerned.

"I didn't realize what was happening at first. I'd never felt anything like it before. All conscious thought stopped, and the electric throbbing between my legs intensified until it became my entire world. I felt my sex opening, inner muscles clenching, and my blood roaring through me like a freight train until I was enveloped in a delicious rush of sensation. Sparks of pure white light exploded behind my closed eyes, and I came, moaning, crying out with joy. I was very happy for a while after that."

"Sadly, Paul was less thrilled about my orgasm than I. And when I shared with him how happy I was to experience such a powerful one from his talented fingers—he informed me that the orgasm I'd just experienced was the wrong kind!"

Jake smirked. "So the old man didn't dig it when he caught on you didn't come when his dick was in you but did when he played with your clit or went down on you. Did he *love* going down on you, by the way?"

I considered the question. "I wonder. I mean he did it, sometimes. But no, he didn't do it like he *loved* it, and he usually stopped before I could come. I think he felt that oral sex was a part of foreplay, strictly intended to get me aroused. After that came the "real thing" as he called it. *That's* when I was supposed to come." I shrugged and threw up my hands.

"I think what he most wanted was to time his orgasm with mine—simultaneous, like you read about in the women's magazines. So what he'd do was hang over me, whispering, 'Are you close yet, baby, are you close yet?' And Jake, that little whisper would freeze my blood, ending right then and there, any chance in a million I might have had of getting off. Finally, he'd finish without me."

"I waited as long as I could," he'd say like he was in line for sanctification.

My inability to climax during intercourse confounded me. I tried and tried, but it just didn't happen. I became tormented about this defect in my sexual responsiveness, wondering if other women had this experience, but had no one to ask. I finally read a book by a Dr. Marie Bonaparte, the only female psychotherapist I could find, a Freudian no less—who claimed that clitoral orgasms were experienced by immature women, who were incapable of achieving orgasm through penile penetration. Vaginal orgasms, the good doctor stated firmly, were the *correct* way for an adult woman to come.

The whole business began to drive me nuts.

I sighed. "Anyway, at that point I gave up and began faking orgasms so well not even my husband knew for sure. I bought myself a vibrator—which was *always* patient with me, used it in secret, and attempted to live happily ever after. It was one solution."

"All that time you never stepped out on him? Never checked out another man?" Jake was amazed. In his world, this was unusual behavior.

"Never did," I said, staring out the window. "There were opportunities; that painting professor at the university for instance; he really attracted me, and I could tell he felt the attraction too. But fool that I was I played it straight! Everything in my upbringing taught me monogamy was synonymous with decency. Actually, I didn't have sex with another man until Paul took off with a multi-orgasmic wonder who could come with a cock in her cunt. Since then, I've checked out, well, almost everyone."

"Tell me, sweetheart," Jake asked, curiously, "what are you looking for?"

What was I looking for? "I'm looking for...well it's like..." I stopped, frustrated, took a deep breath and exhaled sharply. "What I mean to say is I'm like that other Dorothy, from Kansas, who was on her way to ask the Wizard to grant her dearest wish. Off down the Yellow Brick Road I go in search of a vaginal orgasm, and man, I hope that Wizard can make me come."

I'd said enough. Jake stopped my words with a kiss. His hand moved between my legs, arousing me, smiling in triumph when I moaned, and continued his touch in a steady rhythm. I moaned again as I moved into the cloud, saw the sparks and the lights behind my eyes, and exploded with the pure joy of it.

"I wonder who got to decide the right way to come," I asked later.

"Some damn fool old man who wanted his ego stroked," Jake said, laughing. "How the crap can there be a right way to come, as long as both people get satisfied? What you need to do, Dorothy is relax, feel what you can feel, and assure yourself that whatever you're feeling, right now in this moment, is okay."

I stared at him with appreciation. I hadn't expected to find a sex object who was a philosopher as well. "Is that a profound truth?" I teased.

"One of the profoundest," he said, gravely. "Always remember: yesterday's gone; tomorrow's not here yet. Live in the moment."

Yesterday's gone. Tomorrow's not here yet. Live in the moment. Yes!

It was no easy task letting my inhibitions go. After all, they'd been with me a long time and were reluctant to leave. The little bastards were doomed, though, from the day I met Jake, and they knew it. Together we hacked away at them with methodical precision and steel-like determination—until one by one they did Custer's last stand and expired, leaving me another step closer to being free.

I resisted him though, every step of the way, with intellectual arguments and phony ladylike pretenses—which, lucky for me, Jake ignored. If he didn't understand the concept of sin, he didn't understand shame either. He was the mad prophet of the bedroom with second sight into my secret fantasies— and rarely took no for an answer.

"Let me take you on a journey into a fantasy," he'd say, and my hang-ups would clutch each other in mortal terror, wondering who was the next to die.

"Oh Jake, really," I'd say in a superior tone of voice, letting him know, right then and there, that what he'd suggested was humiliating, degrading, and inherently wrong.

"Oh Jake, really, my ass," he'd say. "Don't play lady with me, because I'm no gentleman and wouldn't appreciate it. I'm a low life son of a bitch, and the woman I want is a fucking *slut!*"

"Okay, sweetheart," I'd say grinning, "Show me how to be a slut."

So, we played, and the fantasies revealed themselves. Some were as good as I imagined—like the one involving Kama Sutra Oil, my vibrator and an assortment of sex toys. And, if Jake got off by pushing me to my outer limits, then, by god, he got off that night—slaughtering at least three of my strongest inhibitions, despite customary protests, and with my full cooperation.

Other fantasies, it turned out, were better left to fantasy, like the police handcuffs borrowed from Jake's friend, Barry, who was into the bondage scene. I didn't recall ever having a fantasy about having sex while wearing police handcuffs—silk scarves, maybe—but agreed to try them anyway. They were hard and cold; mostly, they hurt my wrists.

"You win some, you lose some," Jake said, unlocking me. "It's a learning process."

But Jake's conversation is not intellectually stimulating, you say? And somewhat on the crude side, with portions of the script lifted directly from a porno flick? And did I respond to it, modern feminist woman that I was? Oh yes, I did. I responded, in fact, with an eagerness and passion that surprised and impressed me.

Frigid woman my ass, I thought. I'm going to be one hot number before I'm through.

"Thanks to Jake," I wrote to Carla, "I'm learning what makes me tick in bed and am no longer afraid to share the information. I've come a long way from the days when an orgasm was a monthly event, like my period."

"Actually, I've not yet had an orgasm during intercourse no matter what position we've tried, but I am a glass-half-full person and remain optimistic. Sometimes though, nasty little demons, hangers-on from the 1950s, escape from wherever I keep them hidden and torment me, singing *"nah, nah, nah, nah, nah,"* in a high-pitched, sing-song-like whine. *"Real women have vaginal orgasms and you can't!"*

"They rattle my cage, but I'm gaining confidence every day. 'Get lost, demons!' I tell them, and they beat a hasty retreat. Someday, I'll make them be gone for good."

My time spent with Jake was developing nicely into a perfect, contemporary relationship. We laid no claims on each other, no strings, no muss, and no fuss. Our times together were wild and crazy—and depending on how one chose to view them, good clean fun or slightly depraved.

Being a perfect stranger from the start, Jake never cramped my style with other men. On the contrary, in the interest of my sexual liberation, he felt I was wise in sampling all the men I cared to. Far from being jealous, he enjoyed nothing more than a blow-by-blow description of my sexual encounters and inspired me to branch out and literally, embrace all types of men.

So, for my next affair, I chose door number three, yes ladies and gentlemen, Joel, the hippie artist from Brooklyn, New York! I chose him because he was a genuinely funny man, an unofficial comedian in the Woody Allen tradition, complete with a stressed relationship with his mother. Joel was short and stocky, with an olive complexion and dark wavy hair. True to his birth sign, Cancer, he was drawn to bodies of water, and prone to having sex in the old, claw-footed tub in his bathroom, and sometimes serving me home cooked meals in the tub, as well.

He was thirty-two, a talented, penniless painter who lived on a small inheritance while living his dream of being an artist. His idea of taking me out to dinner was to attend art openings in elegant San Francisco galleries, where free food and wine were offered. He also knew the best places in the city for a nutritious and filling happy hour. I found him completely ridiculous and oddly endearing at the same time

Dedicated to his art, he slept on a mattress in his walk-in closet to save space in his basement apartment, in a Fillmore Street Victorian. I later told Harmony that although this lacked a romantic image, it did have a certain back to the womb appeal. Anyway, the whole set up appealed to my sense of humor, and by the time he finished going down on me, I knew we would be lifetime friends.

Not all my playmates turned out to be talented lovers. Take, for instance, the fiasco with Wes, the briefcase carrying executive in a Brook's Brother's suit who referred to the women he lusted after as "young ladies." We met at a *Control Your Destiny* seminar at the Metaphysical Center, near Union Square. Billed as an adventure in self-awareness, the event was presented by an ultra-serene spiritual type, whose qualifications were listed as psychic, tarot reader, and primal therapist. "Your life *will be* what you *will it to be*," she said, while Wes and I took notes and made meaningful eye contact. Later, over coffee, I learned he was conservative to the core; passionate about position, possessions, titles, and suits. He planned on buying a more luxurious car after his next salary increase.

"Cool," I said, hoping I sounded appropriately impressed while picturing his cock in my mind.

He took me to a restaurant overlooking the Pacific. We dined on stuffed Dover sole, mushroom wild rice, and chocolate mousse with raspberries. The meal was a pure sensory pleasure.

After dinner was another story. In his upscale flat, on his king-sized waterbed, Wes proved himself clueless about pleasing a woman. I should have known when he gulped down his dinner, I thought, sadly, recalling Jake's theory that people have sex the way they eat.

For openers he pulled me close, parting my lips almost forcibly with the pressure of his tongue, before sliding said tongue halfway down my throat. I attempted to guide him when he went down on me, but I doubt written instructions would have helped. "Yes! Now go slow," I moaned when he finally found my clit, but he didn't listen and polished off foreplay in three minutes flat. All too soon I found myself gasping for breath—while two hundred pounds of man rose and fell on me, in no particular rhythm at all. I've made a mistake, I thought, and take full responsibility for it but, by god, I refuse to be suffocated! "Lean on your elbows," I said aloud.

"What?" he asked, from the depths of passion.

"Lean on your elbows. You are suffocating me."

Shocked, he raised his torso, but came a minute later and was dead weight again. Using all my strength I heaved him off me, gulping in air. Oblivious, he kissed me, bruising my lip with his teeth, overwhelmed, no doubt, by the wonder of what he thought we'd shared.

"The problem was," Jake said later, "that man was performing. You were just along for the ride. See, a guy like him make the same moves no matter which woman he's with. He does whatever feels good to *him* and then *demands* that she like it." Jake laughed. "In other words, he's a selfish son of a bitch."

"Now, a good lover knows how to get in tune with the woman he's with. In fact, he gets *his* pleasure from giving *her* what she needs and wants. I know these things," he explained, "because I hear them from women all the time. They open up to me because they know I'm a great lover of women—and a great lover, as well."

"See, Dorothy, I'm a selfish son of a bitch myself," he continued. "I love women to respond to me, so I respond to them. Then, their pleasure becomes mine, and I get double pleasure. And. Sweetheart," he grinned, "I'm in it *strictly* for the pleasure."

Clever man, I thought, to understand the basic principle that you've got to give to get. I gazed at him, and he stared back at me. We exchanged knowing looks. "Hey, you selfish-son of a bitch," I said, "why don't you get into me—strictly for the pleasure, of course."

"It'll be my pleasure," Jake said, and it was mine too.

Perfect Strangers

Perfect Stranger Encounter #5

Three-Way

My first experience with three-way sex was at Sutro Bathhouse, San Francisco's only co-ed bathhouse, located in the steamy, South of Market. I was with Jake that night, my perfect stranger—a man with boundless sexual energy and a twisted imagination, who defied all standards of gentlemanly behavior I'd been brought up to expect—and unfailingly focused on what I wanted and needed in bed.

"So, my dear," he inquired one evening after picking me up at my place and escorting me to his truck, "do you happen to recall the fantasy you whispered in my ear the other night, about having sex with two men at once in a public place?"

"Sex with two men at once? In a public place? I said that?" I felt my face flush, and my voice rose up a notch on the word 'public.'

Jake regarded me silently, brows raised and his head cocked to one side, letting the idea sink in. "Come on, sweetheart," he said. "You know you want it, so let's make it happen."

121

Sutro Bathhouse was located in an innocuous Victorian on a tree-lined block near Harrison Street. We were required to fill out a membership card in the front office when we entered the place and to leave our photo IDs at the front desk. I was uneasy about the whole business because it seemed so *intentional,* like some sort of commitment to what would go on inside—and was I really that committed, after all?

Jake, sensing my mood, flashed his lop-sided grin by way of encouragement. As always he made me feel warm and safe and acquiescent, and as we walked off to the dressing rooms to exchange our clothes for bath towels, I grinned back at him and trusted that it would be okay.

It was like a coming-out party, that's how Jake said to think of it—a rite of passage, so to speak, bridging the Grand Canyon-sized gap between those of us who have experienced group sex, and those who have not.

Rock music greeted us as we stepped inside the club. Our first stop that evening was the lounge, a room furnished with beat-up old chairs and couches and a table with refreshments at the far end. We stood looking around. The place smelled of wood and cigarette smoke and chlorine from the hot tub on the fenced-in back patio. Feeling a bit overexposed, I grounded myself with iced tea and various munchies, while the Rolling Stones played on the jukebox near the door. A few towel-clad couples were in the room when we arrived, along with a handful of single men who eyed me with interest—like wolves who'd just spotted a sheep.

Jake nodded a cool 'hi' when one of them caught his eye, angling for an invitation to join us, but made no introductions. "That man's hot for you," he informed me in a whisper. "You wouldn't enjoy him; he looks way too uptight for you. We'll shop around for someone mellow."

Two single men near us were sampling the refreshments and discussing last week's major bathhouse event. It seems that on Thursday a couple arrived and let the word out that the lady was living out an erotic fantasy, and willing to take on every man in the house. She began with her own old man, it wasn't clear why—good form perhaps, or maybe he got the motor running just right. Anyway, she and her old man took one of the small private rooms upstairs. Interested men formed a line outside the door.

"I was fifth in line," complained one of the men, biting into a brownie. He was blond with thinning hair and a narrow chest. "Fifth in line; do you have any idea what that's like?"

"Pretty messed up," the other man said with a knowing nod.

That's an understatement, I thought, sipping my iced tea and visualizing the scenario. "How long was the line?" I asked, suppressing a laugh.

The first man turned to me with interest. "She took on *nine men* that night," he said, in a confidential tone. "With her old man there in the room watching every move that was made."

"There were actually thirteen in the line," the second man said," but only nine got laid. There were still four guys waiting their turn when she said she was tired and was going home. Some people were very disappointed," he said, with disapproval.

"Yes," I said, shaking my head, straight-faced, "it's so hard to find people you can depend on these days."

Jake listened in on the story with interest. I imagined he was sorry to have missed that little scene. "Wouldn't I have loved being number one *and* number nine," he reflected wistfully.

"Don't feel so bad," I soothed, as we finished our tea and went off to explore. "Maybe you'll catch her next performance."

Porno flicks were being shown in a darkened room off the lounge, and we peeked in to take a look.

"Hey, check that one out," Jake pointed to the screen. A busty blonde lay seductively on an animal print bedspread. Approaching her was a muscular young man, with an abundance of body hair, and the largest penis I'd ever seen.

"Ever had one like that?" Jake inquired.

"Not like *that*." I stared, mesmerized by the image. God, it was big.

"Wouldn't you love one like that, sweetheart,"

Jake teased. "Think you could take it all up that pretty cunt of yours?"

"Maybe..." I said, grinning, "But I'd probably need plastic surgery afterward."

"Come on, Dorothy." Jake said, putting an arm around me. "I want us to check out the main orgy room; that's the best place in the house to get down and do it."

Curious, I followed him into the large, sunken, dimly lit space. The middle part of the floor was strewn with mattresses that were so far unoccupied. Several men and women were sitting or lying on oversized throw pillows that lined the perimeters of the room.

"Look up," Jake said from the center of the space.

I did as he said, and tilting my head back, gazed at my wide-eyed reflection in the mirrored ceiling. I understood then why people were gathering. They were the audience, and this was the stage. And center-stage, I thought, we have Dorothy, here tonight in the interest of sexual liberation, and Jake, sexual liberator, par excellence. The audience cheers wildly, as Jake calls for a volunteer from the audience.

And sex is a spectator sport.

"Come here to me, woman, I want you," Jake said in a hoarse whisper, dropping his towel and revealing his erection. He stared at me intently. "Down on your knees. Blow me. Take it all."

Well, the fact is I did—by relaxing my throat

muscles and breathing evenly through my nose—I licked and sucked and nibbled at his cock, reveling in my power to please him; his balls hot and heavy in my hands. Shocks of pleasure coursed through me. My clit pulsed. My inner muscles clenched, making me moan. My eyes closed and the audience around me vanished. My persistent pirate fantasy appeared in my brain. I was in a richly appointed, ship's cabin on the open ocean, a highborn lady, kidnapped and held captive by the pirate captain himself.

"Remove your clothes," he ordered, and his tone commanded my obedience.

There was a second pirate in the captain's cabin. He watched me strip silently, with predatory eyes and waited his turn.

My eyes reopened when Jake laid me back on a mattress and began to caress me: feeling, kissing, rubbing, stroking all my right places, seemingly unaware we were being watched. I was aware of it though. The feeling was new for me, strange, decadent, forbidden, depraved—but clearly a turn-on. *Exhibitionism becomes you, Dorothy*, I thought, feeling my nipples tighten and a rush of arousal between my legs. I stared up into the mirrors, seeing the entire room—with me, its slim, naked centerpiece, my dark bushy hair spread out over a pillow, gazing wide-eyed at my audience of perfect strangers.

Someone else was touching me. I saw the man's reflection in the mirror before seeing him on the mattress beside me. He was short and stocky, with wide shoulders and coarse, dark hair, and wore only a rubber. He didn't speak. His foot caressed mine, tentatively, questioningly.

So this is how one asks, I thought, Emily Post, take note.

Something about the man and his manner appealed to me. I didn't move my foot away, and encouraged, he sat down beside me, lightly stroking my shoulder and then my breast. I looked up into his eyes wondering, briefly, who he was but decided that didn't matter. Hello, sweetheart, I thought and smiled a welcome.

Jake glanced up from between my legs. His look was a question. I nodded my okay, and he did the same. The man leaned in closer and took my nipple into his mouth.

If the truth be told, in spite of the unbridled passions zapping around the room that night—I got off more on the *idea* of what I was doing, than the actual doing itself. I observed the entire event unfold before me like a film. The stranger attempted to please me, but I couldn't come with him, I came later, alone with Jake, when he played with my clit.

We wound up the evening in the hot tub, which was relaxing after our earlier exertions. Jake got into a spirited conversation with two women sitting near us about how negatively sexual pleasure is viewed by society and how royally messed up that is—but I was tired and introspective and sat soaking beside him without joining in.

"So all things considered," Jake said later, driving us home in the early hours of the morning, "what are your feelings on what you experienced tonight?"

I was silent a minute before answering, replaying the events of the evening in my mind: the nudity, the mirrored ceiling, the live audience, and the dark-eyed stranger, whose name I didn't know, and with whom I'd been intimate, and what judgments Paul would pass on my choice of entertainment—and how life takes us in directions we never imagined we'd go.

"Another fantasy heard from," I said, shrugging my shoulders, "What else can I say?"

Perfect Stranger Encounter #6

The Foursome

I suspected we'd end up as a threesome when Jake suggested spending the evening at his friend Richard's flat in the Outer Mission. I'd have been surprised if we didn't, the way he kept assuring me I'd like the guy. In fact, "Built like a bull and loves oral sex," were his exact words.

"Sounds like an offer I can't refuse," I said, and a date was set for Thursday evening, around nine.

I was cool and confident about my upcoming sexual adventure until Jake informed me, when we were almost to Richards's house, that plans had changed. Instead of three, there would be *four* tonight.

"*Four?*" I echoed, visualizing the possibilities. "But Jake, aren't we rushing things?" I asked, looking up at him. "I've just worked up to three, and now you want four? Who's the other man? Do I know him?"

Jake was beside me at the wheel of his Chevy pickup, driving toward upper Folsom Street. He eyed me, nonchalantly, gauging my response. "It's not a him, sweetheart, it's a *her*. A beautiful female friend of Richard's and mine. She's a Libra," he said, by way of reassurance. "You'll like her a lot."

We both knew my protests were mere formalities. But *what do I do with the other woman*, I wondered, and *what might she do with me?* I worried the questions around in my mind until we pulled up to a faded, brown building on a tree-lined street. The wind was blowing like mad when we got out of the car. We wrapped our jackets tight around us to stay warm and rushed up the stairs to the porch.

The woman's name was Clear Beginning—a San Francisco name if I ever heard one. She opened the door with a welcoming smile and showed us into a dimly-lit flat. "Richard's in the shower, he'll join us soon," she said. "Please sit down. What can I offer you?"

Richard's spacious living room was sparsely furnished with two brown upholstered chairs, a brown couch, and several large pillows, also brown. Old oak bookcases along the walls were fully lined with books. When he wasn't having hot sex with perfect strangers, Richard, evidently, liked to read.

While Jake checked out the book titles, Clear served us tea, seating herself on a chair with her cup. I curled up on the sofa with mine and observed her. She was girl-next-door pretty, trim, graceful, with a blond,

Jewish Afro, and wearing a filmy purple dress and silver hoop earrings. Her smile put me at ease, and I smiled back.

"You two have lots in common," Jake said. He settled his six-foot frame on the sofa, flung an arm around me, and launched into the details of Clear's life story.

She was forty-two, with a daughter, twelve, who lived with her and spent summers and holidays with her dad. Clear came from an upper crust, Philadelphia family, and was married for a long time to a Jewish doctor. She had innumerable sexual hang-ups, and never once had an orgasm the whole time she was married—except for three times when she had sex with the shrink her husband was paying to find out why she couldn't come. Clear was very happy about her three orgasms but experienced such guilt about screwing her shrink that she developed a number of new hang-ups, and took them all to a new shrink. And so life went on.

Then, one spring morning in 1971, she woke and knew in her gut it was time to change her life. She closed out her bank account, packed her kid and her clothes into her station wagon, and drove off into the dawning of the Age of Aquarius. When she reached San Francisco, she discovered an exciting new lifestyle, renamed herself, and started over. Five years later, she owned a successful Haight Street clothing business, had a great relationship with her daughter, and sexually speaking was having a blast.

"I hear you're from New York, Dorothy. How did you find your way here and into the hands of this *unsavory* character?" Clear grinned at Jake and poured us more tea.

"A tornado blew me here," I said. "Like Dorothy, in Oz."

She nodded. "You remind me of myself when I first met Jake. Imagine: a runaway wife, searching for my misplaced sexuality. And I found *him*." She raised her teacup in salutation.

Jake flashed his lopsided grin. "Her problem was she was hung up on being a lady." He turned to me. "But I taught her to be a slut."

She blushed but didn't deny it. We exchanged looks. "Slut lessons," I said, arching my brows, "Of course."

"We met in Golden Gate Park one night," she said. "I was out walking, and Jake stopped to caution me about weird men wanting sex. She shrugged her shoulders and smiled. "What can I say? The man beats therapy. I hope you're up for sharing. Men like him are in short supply."

"What's that? A man shortage?" a deep male voice asked.

"Richard, come and meet Dorothy," Clear said.

Richard was in his late forties, tall, very thin, and looked like a man who could play a duke in a British movie. There was elegance about him, even in jeans and an old velvet smoking jacket, and his fine-boned face bore the stamp of some grave disappointment. He sat beside Clear, sipping wine, not tea, and the four of us sat in the brown living room looking each other over.

The lights were dim, and the soul-stirring sounds of Ravi Shankar came from the stereo. Clear rummaged in her purse and produced a bag of pot. "Lebanese blond," she said. The pipe was passed. We toked. We talked. We all got high. My body was buzzing and felt as though I was floating. I spaced out for a while, with images meandering through my mind like a triple feature movie. When I was present again, I saw everyone else was almost naked—Jake in jeans and a leather vest, and Richard in his smoking jacket. Clear wore dangling, silver earrings and nothing else. Her small breasts were high and firm with dark, prominent nipples.

In my absence, a vote has been taken, and the motion for an orgy has passed.

Well, well...I was bold before, but now I was nervous. Everyone was looking at me—at all my clothes. I felt like a model in a fashion show. And here's Dorothy in low-cut black, with knee-high boots—and the gold heart-shaped locket her daddy gave her when she was sixteen.

I eyed Richard. No kidding, the man was endowed. He eyed me too, his gaze lingering on my stiffened nipples, visible beneath the fabric of my blouse. The desire in his eyes triggered mine.

Three naked people watched me intently. One

was a woman; beautiful, smooth, curvy, and undeniably hot. But what are her intentions toward me? What if she wants to do something I don't? Can I refuse without spoiling the mood for everyone? Well, Dorothy, you wanted experience, and now here you are. So off with your clothes, and lay back baby, and enjoy it!

I felt very center stage as I began my striptease. Jake nodded approval. Clear smiled like she knew my thoughts. Richard watched me with hungry eyes. Slowly, I unbuttoned my blouse, unhooked my lacy black bra, and unzipped my skirt, letting it drop to the floor at my feet. I stepped from it naked and with conscious seduction, raised my arms in salutation, and made a small bow with my head.

Let the festivities begin.

For openers, Richard joined me on the sofa, with Clear and Jake on the overstuffed chair. Looks like she worked through *her* frigidity issues, I thought, watching enviously as she surrendered to pleasure without self-consciousness. Jake's hands roamed her body, massaging her lower back, and hips, and inner thighs, making her moan. He watched me while he did this. I smiled, and he nodded, cupping her breasts in his hands. Taking each of her nipples between a thumb and a forefinger, he gave a sharp little squeeze. Clear gasped with pleasure, and I connected with their excitement, moaning in response as though I'd been touched too.

My body felt thick and molten with wanting. I turned to Richard, ready for action. His eyes widened, and he pulled me close to him, kissing me, his tongue exploring my mouth. He had a good rich taste and a musky, male smell.

"Yes," I murmured, when he pressed me back against a pillow and, kneeling, placed his face between my legs. Quickly, I realized that my personal acid test had been passed—the man knew how to go down. Smiling, I lay back and relaxed. Jake, fondling Clear, watched me like a director watches his actors onstage. I saw the familiar gleam of triumph in his eyes—before I closed mine and went with the feelings.

They were going at it when I opened my eyes again, banging away like nothing else mattered. Jake plunged into her repeatedly, their bellies connecting with a wet, slapping sound. Watching them turned me on.

I turned to Richard, ready for more. He eyed me hungrily but made no move. I saw he was soft. "What's up?" I blurted, without thinking.

His eyes were pained and apologetic, "Obviously, not me, love. Sorry, I get nervous the first time I'm with a woman."

"Me too," I said, looking at Clear, and we both laughed.

It was okay, after that. I went down on the man with all my acquired expertise. Moaning, he hardened, growing so hugely that I widened my jaws, snakelike, to accommodate him. I saw Clear's eyes widen in appreciation.

Then we all lay on the rug and did it side by side with eight hands roaming in all directions. Clear's silky thigh pressed mine, and I didn't move away. But then we changed partners again. I moaned in delight as Jake's familiar hardness filled me. "You feel so good," I whispered, squeezing down on him for all I was worth and hanging on for the ride.

Later, both men kissed and fondled me. Clear looked on smiling. Now and then I felt her light, non-intrusive touch and we exchanged smiles. Then, the men moved aside, and she kissed my mouth. Her lips were soft, and I smelled the sweet fragrance of her hair. I hesitated, turned on by the idea of what we were doing, but realizing I didn't desire her the way I desired men.

Still, I offered no resistance, and my eyes closed as her hot, moist mouth glided between my thighs. She teased my clit with her tongue, moving it in a steady rhythm, while her slim, graceful hands stroked and massaged. My god, she knows what she's doing, I thought, as my orgasm built and came on hard, in a rush of exquisite energy that enveloped me and made me cry out.

She was gazing down at me when I opened my eyes. She bent to kiss my mouth, and I could taste my excitement on her lips. Our arms entwined and the softness of her breasts rubbed against mine. An unfamiliar excitement began to mount.

"Lie back," I took her by the shoulders and pushed her against the pillows. "Let me pleasure you."

I made her come. I wasn't sure I could pull it off at first. Such unfamiliar terrain; no wonder men are intimidated, I thought, kneeling, gazing at her wet, swollen opening, parting her lips, seeking her clit.

Her clit looked like a tiny cock, peeking from her silky pubic hair. I teased it first, barely touching it with my tongue. She groaned, hips grinding, while I explored her, paying close attention to her moans and the intake of her breath—the way Jake paid attention to mine.

"Yes!" she moaned, when I flicked her hard little kernel with my tongue. Her breathing quickened, and I slipped two fingers inside her, feeling her inner muscles clench, and her long slim fingers entwine in my hair. "Yes! Yes!" she screamed, tensing, limbs stiffening as she came hard.

The men joined in again after that, and as Jake said, no worries, we were just four beautiful people getting down and doing it together. And we all loved each other so much.

Perfect Strangers

Part Four—1976/1977

A Gaggle Of Geese, A Stable Of Studs

Dear Carla,

In your last letter, you asked how I feel deep inside, after two years of being on my own. Excellent question and one to which I've given considerable thought. Here's what I've come up with. Let me know if it makes sense to you.

The other day I stood before my mirror—not unusual in itself since I'm always in the process of getting gorgeous for somebody. But I was feeling analytical about my appearance and observed myself closely to determine what men saw when they looked at me.

I saw a shapely woman, Carla, more mature than I'd realized and no longer a girl. Not beautiful, but vivid and very alive with a look in her eyes saying what? That I was bold, desirable, and available? An erotic adventuress and a great lay? And tough, don't even doubt it. Not to be trifled with.

I looked closer, and yes, there was something else—a hint perhaps, from deep within those green irises, of a deep and bitter hurt.

So, sometimes I feel terrific, high as a kite on the excitement of being alive. I get out of bed in the morning ready and willing to face the new day. I feel good about my life, my apartment, even my parenting skills, and proud of providing a clean, comfortable home for my sons, all on my own, and being in charge of my life with no one to answer to. That's worth a lot to me.

But sometimes I start thinking about Paul, remembering our life together, and how I spent years feeling unsatisfied and put down—and of the painful way our marriage ended, and how now, thanks to his irresponsibility, I'm stuck in a dead end job supporting two kids for years to come. Alone, with no one to love me best of all!

When I think like that, I loathe Paul with an intensity that frightens me. But on some level I don't understand, I fear, in spite of everything, I might still love him. Oh to hell with him! He's out of my life and good riddance. I'm having more fun with a pack of perfect strangers than I ever had with him.

Speaking of perfect strangers, Jake is alive, well, and available to take me out into the night for evenings of *wild sexual excess*. That has a nice ring to it, don't you think? Let's hear it for Jake. We don't love each other—but we serve each other's purposes well.

There's a new man in my life named Richard. He's a forty-year-old, occasionally published poet whose work is far out and ahead of his time. Jake introduced us, and we hit it off right away. We're having an intellectual/sexual relationship, which basically means we read poetry and discuss literature before we have sex.

How did we meet, you ask? We met at a mini-orgy at his house involving Jake and me, and...well...another woman. Her name is Clear Beginning, and she's self-confident, successful, and very cool. We liked each other right off and have been developing a friendship since that night we met. She has strong opinions on what she calls the mythical vaginal orgasm and believes the clitoris is the true source of female pleasure.

Meeting her was an educational experience for me—and an insightful one. That night, Carla, I learned the truth about my bisexual tendencies, and although I loved my experience with Clear, and have no regrets about it, I think I'm basically straight. What a shame, since Jake and Clear assure me that the true New Age person will be bisexual. But I learned another truth the night I met her that's good to know—if you close your eyes and focus on the sensation while receiving oral sex, pleasure overrides everything.

I met a man recently, from Venice, Italy, in San Francisco on a business trip; a vigorous, high energy Aries lover. We were instantly attracted, and that same evening, I enjoyed his company in bed. A cultured man, he'd studied art history in his country, and told fascinating tales of life in the famous city of canals, romantic gondolas, and ancient buildings that were works of art in themselves. Before he returned home, we discussed my visiting him in Venice, but I knew that wouldn't happen. He was passing through on his to way somewhere else, and it was fun while it lasted and no more than that. Funny though, I felt sad when we parted—not because he was leaving, but because I knew I wouldn't miss him when he was gone.

Thanks for your patience when my mom called to grill you on the state of my wellbeing. She keeps writing me plaintive little notes filled to over-flowing with her fears and concerns. I keep assuring her I'm okay, but she refuses to believe anyone living a 'wild' lifestyle in a decadent city like San Francisco can be okay. She'd love nothing more, she tells me each time we write or talk on the phone, than for me to move back East to be near her, so she can see her grandkids more than a once or twice a year.

She's upset, poor lady, that in spite of her best efforts, her only daughter didn't turn out like she expected. I didn't turn out like I expected either, but am doing my best with the woman I turned out to be.

To answer your question, of course, I don't mind your offering opinions or advice. It's refreshing to have a dose of sanity arrive in my mailbox at regular intervals, like a care package. Maybe someday, I'll know what to do with it.

By the way, I took a week off from work

recently and drove the boys down to Disneyland for some wholesome, family fun. We stayed in a motel right across the highway from the entrance, and Brad and Doug had the time of their lives with Mickey Mouse and Company for the next few days. We were the first patrons to enter in the morning and the last to leave at night—and you are, in fact, talking to a woman who went on the Pirates of the Caribbean ride, nine consecutive times. I was half-dead from exhaustion by the time we headed home, but honestly, I had a great time too.

Thanks for the photos of your family vacation at Lake Ontario. Now the boys are pestering me to take them speed-boating, and think it would be cool to learn to water ski.

Well, goodbye for now. I've enclosed some photos of us in Disneyland. The boys are really getting big, aren't they?

Write soon. I love you.
Dorothy

P.S.—Did you ever stop to consider that if this world is one large padded cell, then we must be the inmates?

Perfect Strangers

CHAPTER SEVEN

My waitress, Diane, was out sick one foggy July morning. The coffee house was packed. I rushed around, filling in, pouring coffee, toasting bagels, and helping out my other waitress, Anne, who was stressed. A young couple with a guitar and a banjo came in asking for breakfast in exchange for live music, and I happily agreed. The music brought more people in. It was afternoon when the stream of customers slowed and I sat at the counter with coffee and a bagel. That's when I noticed the blued-eyed, broad-shouldered guy in a motorcycle jacket at the next table. He caught my eye, smiled, and said hello.

Stuart looked to be in his mid-thirties and was attractive in a weathered, Marlboro man kind of way, but he turned out to be manly, not macho, which was oddly appealing. He was single and lived in the neighborhood, and earned a decent living restoring and painting San Francisco Victorians. A long-time motorcycle rider, he spent many weekends riding with friends.

"I'm glad I came here today, Dorothy," he said before leaving. "I usually go to the café at Masonic, but today something said to come here." Stuart towered over me at six-foot-two. He had a sweet, shy smile. "You'll be seeing me again."

"I am *so* not a morning person," I said, a week later, as yawning, I straddled the passenger seat of Stuart's enormous Harley, a safety helmet on my head. "The kids slept over with friends last night. I could be sleeping late. I can't believe you've talked me into this."

Stuart smiled. "Once we get going, Dorothy, you'll understand why bikers get up before the sun." He turned the ignition key, the motor came alive beneath us, and we began our ride. Wrapping my arms around Stuart's waist, I pressed up against him and hung on as we headed west toward the ocean. On Ocean Beach, I looked back at the sun rising in the east over the sleeping city.

"The world looks so beautiful," I said, "so peaceful, so still, like a world without heartache. Thanks for inviting me along."

We ate breakfast at Lou's café overlooking the beach, gazing out at the open ocean, delighting in the screaming of seagulls and the waves crashing against Seal Rock, below. Lingering over our eggs, toast, and coffee, we kept up a relaxed flow of conversation. For a guy, I thought, Stuart understands me surprisingly well.

Brad and Doug were thrilled to learn I'd made a friend who rode a motorcycle and became his lifetime buddies when he took each of them for a ride a week later. They insisted I take pictures of them sitting astride the bike with helmets on to send to Carla's kids.

"This guy is cool, Mom," Brad said.

"And he's not just pretending to like us to please you," said Doug.

I had to agree. Stuart was a cool guy, but of course he was a friend, not a lover—which set him apart from all the rest.

He began dropping by a few times a week, sometimes taking one of us biking or all of us to the movies. Sometimes he stopped in at the coffeehouse while I was working and hung out with me. More than once, he showed up around dinner time with containers of Chinese food and spent the evening visiting with the boys and me.

And so I came to depend on him to fix little things around the flat, or to rap with the boys about *manly* subjects they weren't willing to discuss with me, or to spend a quiet hour over coffee now and then to share thoughts and feelings.

"Stuart's got good energy," I told my women friends. "He's a Capricorn, solid, steady, and dependable. I think he's a man I can trust."

"A rare man indeed," Harmony said, snidely. She was having power-struggles with her latest lover and was on edge.

"Have you had sex with him yet?" Clear asked.

"No, and I'd just as soon keep it that way. I have more than enough lovers, but can always use more friends."

Stuart made an interesting contrast to Jake, who was all about sex—a human manual on 743 ways to experience sexual sensation. Like the night he got the brainstorm to attach the rubber dildo to a wire coat hanger and bend the wire into a homemade crank. He slid the dildo in, turned the crank, and the thing kind of squirmed around inside me.

"How does it feel?" he wanted to know. "Like you're getting it on with a snake?"

I stifled a laugh. "Actually, it feels more like I'm a kitchen sink being fixed by a plumber."

Jake gave me a look, informing me I was being middle-class again; blocking my feelings, because I was uptight about committing a perverted sexual act.

"Give it a chance," he said. "Just lie there and experience the sensation." So, I lay there with this flesh colored roto-rooter inside me, experiencing the sensations; thinking he was nuts and I was right there with him when he stopped abruptly. "Far out!" he said, bowled over by some great new idea. "Have I got a thought!"

I laughed. "What? Don't tell me you've thought of an encore for this act?"

Jake's eyes gleamed with his new cognition. "Do you realize, Dorothy, that if I attached two dildos to two cranks, and put them into two women, and stuck my cock into a third woman, I could fuck all three at once?"

With Stuart, I talked philosophy. Why are we here? Where are we going? What on earth do we do along the way? We discussed me and my failed marriage, which still weighed heavily on my mind.

"I was an only child of older parents," I said. "They were crazy about me; paid me all kinds of attention, but I always wished for a brother or sister to play with and tell my secrets to. Everyone I knew had at least one other kid in the family. I felt left out of that experience. I didn't make friends easily and spent lots of time alone. I'd draw, write poetry, and was always making little creatures out of sand or mud. I'd talk to them like they were alive.

Stuart smiled, and I imagined he was visualizing me as a dreamy little girl, nurtured by adoring parents, who created fantasy creatures to keep from feeling alone.

"My dad died of cancer the year I was sixteen," I continued. "That was the first terrible thing to happen in my life. It showed me some clear-cut polarity between the *real world*, filled with harsh realities, and my inner world that was rich with fantasies and dreams."

"And you got married not long after that," Stuart said.

"You must have seen this film before. Yes, I met Paul that year. I thought I loved him after we had sex for the first time—but maybe I was simply hot for him and mistook lust for love."

"Anyway, I was de-virginized, engaged, and married before I had a clue as to what I was getting myself into. My mom was freaked out about the whole thing and urged me not to marry until I was older, but I was too young and full of myself to pay attention." I sighed, deeply. "As far as I was concerned, Paul Freed was the love of my life. He was handsome, smart, capable, and told me he was going to be a great writer—and I, oh noble ambition, would be a great writer's wife and live happily ever after, which is where all my troubles began."

Telling my story riled me up inside. Carla said a time would come when it wouldn't bother me anymore, but that time hadn't yet arrived. Avoiding Stuart's eyes, I rose from my chair and paced around my living room, stopping before the bay window to stare out at a foggy night on Haight Street.

"Let me guess what happened next," Stuart said. I could tell from his voice he was grinning. "You signed the contract *before* reading the fine print."

"Right again," I said, grinning. "And when I finally did—man, did I get more than I'd bargained for! We clashed from the start, over small things, mostly. Paul liked being in control. He had a short emotional fuse and controlled me with his anger, so I walked around on eggshells a lot of the time. Still, with my seventeen years of experience at understanding human nature, I put an unpleasant disposition down to creative temperament and kept knocking myself out trying to please him." I turned to Stuart again. "Then I got pregnant, and that was that!"

I turned back to the window. "I was thrilled. We'd be the perfect all-American family—husband and wifey and baby makes three." I shrugged. "I figured everything would work out somehow because we were *in love*, but it turned out that I was wrong."

I stopped, embarrassed by my feelings. I rarely revealed this Dorothy to men. "Hey, listen to me telling you all this emotional stuff. You can't really want to hear this long involved story?"

Stuart nodded, put a pillow behind him, and sat back comfortably on the couch. I curled up in the armchair across from him. Glancing at a framed photo of Brad and Doug's smiling faces on the end table beside me, I continued my story.

"My marriage began to end when I was in my mid-twenties. Using money my Dad left for my education, I signed up for art classes at the Syracuse University's night school. I attended fall, spring and summer classes for two years. When Doug was four, I put him in nursery school and matriculated to the main campus as a full-time student. It was *not* easy doing schoolwork, while cooking, cleaning, shopping, caring for two feisty kids, and catering to a husband who felt his responsibilities ended when he came home from work. Funny, I'd hear other, younger students counting the days until graduation, but I *loved* going to school so much I never wanted it to end."

"I'll show you photos of my artwork." I

scrambled from my chair and rummaged through my desk drawer. "Some of it is stored with my friend Carla back in my old neighborhood; the rest is at my mom's place, in New York. Look." I pointed to an image. "This bowl was thrown on a potter's wheel. Its handles are made from coils of clay. And I hand-built these little animal-like forms from clay slabs, colored with mineral oxides. I feel good about the way the colors and textures worked out, and the way the creature's orange eyes seem to follow you."

Stuart studied the photographs. I had a happy feeling he was connecting with the part of me that made art. "I don't know that much about art, but these look good," he said.

"They *were* good, and I loved making them. I loved creating forms that came alive and stood on their own. My professors thought I was good, too. I got mostly A's, and a few B's, and even won the school's ceramic art competition in my junior year." I shifted my weight and sat up straighter. "I was blown away by winning that award; it did wonders for my ego. I even started imagining I might really *be* an artist—not just some harassed housewife playing with crafts while the kids took a nap."

"And your old man didn't go for it, right?" Stuart shook his head and grinned.

I laughed. "Didn't go for it? Why, he hated the idea the way Nixon hated left-wing radicals. The dream of his life, as I understood it, was to have a wife who found fulfillment in baking cookies for her loved ones, while washing down the walls in her spare time. And there he was, stuck with me wanting to make art every moment I could. Naturally, he got upset."

"What a shame," Stuart said, "for men to fear losing power and control when their women become passionate about a career. They don't stop to think how that career might add more dimension to their women."

"Bravo!" I said, liking him. "May I quote you widely on that?"

"As widely as you like." He looked at the photo again, then at me. "Do you do artwork now, Dorothy?"

I took a deep breath and exhaled, slowly. "Not now... I haven't given up my dream though... But being a working artist takes dedication and focus. I had that once...but my life has been so chaotic these last few years that I haven't..." I fell silent. Discussing the artistic career, I *wasn't* pursuing, was getting me depressed.

"Where's your focus now?"

"You mean besides working for a living and raising two rambunctious sons? Well, I'm having fun; making up for lost time. I'm dating and learning to understand men—then...maybe I won't be so afraid of them." I stopped, abruptly. Did I really say that?

"Do men scare you, then?" Stuart sounded so kind.

"I guess they do…"

It was true. I hated to admit it, but I was afraid of men. Women, with the exception of Cassandra, I saw as sisters, friends to be counted on. But to my mind, men were alien, incomprehensible creatures, capable of taking your affection, loyalty, and freedom, and then hurting you to the core.

But only if I let them, I thought—and I was too wise.

As my mom always told me, "Stay with the crowd, Dorothy, there's safety in numbers." And as my mom *never* told me—there's safety in having sex with perfect strangers, because you don't get in close enough to get hurt.

Although I was a self-declared player now, a hard-nosed realist, if you please, who viewed marriage scornfully as the social plot it was, and monogamy as an outdated joke—secretly I still harbored the hope that a miracle might happen, and I'd meet the perfect stranger who might turn into more than a stranger, and who would prove me wrong.

I observed those of my friends who were in love with eagle eyes, analyzing the quality of their relationships, hoping to be convinced that Prince Charming wasn't dead, but merely sleeping. But as far as I could see, everyone I knew who was in love, was suffering. Love, in my opinion, was a war zone, raging with doubt, desolation, anger, and general mistrust.

For instance, Allison of the open marriage finally fell for one of her lovers, who promptly shrank from her desire for greater intimacy and ran the other way. Conclusion: Love led to pain.

Or Harmony, who found her soul mate in the form of a married man. She wanted all of him, and he promised her Tuesday evenings for years to come. Love led to disappointment.

Even Carla, my one sane friend, was having problems with Ray. As a woman of the 70s, she was drawn to new ways of spicing up their sex life and broached the subject of certain sex toys she'd been thinking about. Ray, who was somewhat stodgy, resisted her efforts to fix what he felt wasn't broken. Love led to frustration.

Steve fell in love with a twenty-five-year-old he met at a nude beach, who demanded he leave Allison and make a 'real marriage' with her. Love led to panic.

Richard was in love with the memory of his ex-wife, who'd left him for another man. Love led to depression.

Joel fell for a conservative and attempted to fit into her world. Love led to dishonesty.

Ain't love grand? I thought, and couldn't help but notice that with all the suffering going on around me, only Clear Beginning, Jake, and I escaped unscathed. We enjoyed everyone and loved no one. We kept ourselves safe that way.

Perfect Strangers

Perfect Stranger Encounter #7

The Gambler

I met Jerry, the gambler, on a sunny August afternoon at Bay Meadows Racetrack. I was standing near the finish line, breathing in the smell of sweaty horses combined with cigarette smoke, beer, and plenty of dust, cheering for a horse destined to come in last. Brad and Doug were with me and also cheering, but for a different horse. Disloyal children, I thought, irritably, crumpling my losing ticket and tossing it in the trash.

"You lost again, Mom! You didn't listen to me. I *said* number six was going to win!" Doug's little face was flushed with excitement at having picked the winning horse. "Brad listened to me, and he won too. You should have listened to me, Mom!"

"Thank you, Doug for your input," I snarled, looking back toward the finish line. And that's when I saw him; the well-dressed black hunk who'd been watching me for the last three races. He caught my eye and smiled—all the proof *I'd* ever need that black was beautiful. I was glad I'd worn my new platform heels and the green velvet pants that showed my ass to perfection.

I scrutinized him, from his polished leather boots to the tightly wound ringlets of his Afro, pausing along the way to check out the expensive wool slacks and jacket. The top buttons of his white silk shirt were left open, revealing smooth, brown skin. He had full, kissable lips, and eyes the color of espresso beans. Well hello, sweetheart, I thought, as my snarl dissolved into a wide, seductive smile. My mind raced a mile a minute, thinking all sorts of female chauvinist pig thoughts.

"Have you picked some winners today?" I asked, starting up a conversation, and he pulled a fistful of tickets from his jacket pocket in response and said, a bit smugly, "I bet horses for a living, baby. It's my business to win."

I was delighted. "You're a professional gambler? I've never met one before."

"Then why don't I tell you all about my profession over dinner, and…?"

"Dinner and?" I broke in, with a lift of my eyebrows. "Now that sounds intriguing."

"I'll bet on that," he said.

Black gambler fantasy, take one. Lights! Camera! Action!

The man's name was Jerry. He was a Sagittarian, the sign that rules good fortune, and appeared to be a naturally lucky man. I bet right along with him after he joined us. To my delight, I won money all afternoon, and Doug decided to become a professional gambler when he grew up. And as we placed our bets and cheered our horses to the finish line and collected our money, little electric jolts of excitement zapped back and forth between us, promising greater glories to come.

My sons observed our interaction, and I wondered if they realized that their mother was seducing a perfect stranger while they studied their racing forms. (I couldn't imagine *my* mother seducing a stranger anywhere at all, no matter *how* perfect he was.) I gave him my phone number before we left the track and drove home, happily speculating on what he'd be like in bed.

"Hey Mom," Brad said in the car.

"Yes, Brad?"

"I've been wondering...how grownups... Well, you know...get together?"

I smiled at him, understanding what he meant. Poor thing; he'd turned thirteen last February, and to put it charitably, was in an awkward stage. He was taller than I, and his voice was in the process of changing. Small, oddly placed tufts of hair were growing haphazardly on his face, interspersed with an occasional pimple, and his skinny neck had grown giraffe-like in proportion to his body. I'd observed that his interest in girls had awakened, although I suspected he was too shy to actually approach one.

"What I mean is..." he took a breath and went on in a determined tone. "Well, how do they let each other know they're interested in, well, you know…each other?"

"If you'd been listening to all those dopey things Mom and that guy, Jerry, told each other at the race track, you'd know," Doug said wisely.

I grinned. "Brad, those are some excellent questions you just asked me, and setting your brother's words of wisdom aside, let me do my best to explain…"

Jerry and I met for dinner in San Francisco the next evening, at the Hyatt Regency Hotel across from the Ferry Building. His eyes lit up when I walked into the restaurant, and I'm sure mine did too. We were seated across from each other at an intimate, candle-lit table, where we flirted and chatted and joked and laughed easily together—as though we'd known each other for longer than two days. Dinner was a heady combination of delicious food and mounting sexual tension that had my nipples standing at attention for the entire meal. We gazed steadily at one another as we ate. Our eyes promised everything.

After dinner, we retired to the spacious, lushly carpeted suite he called his Bay Area home. While he poured Chardonnay at the bar near the refrigerator and set the radio to a pop music station, I sat, cross-legged on the plush, gray sofa that faced the front window looking out at the darkened sky and night lights of the city. I was thinking about relationships—the mysterious variables that made them work or not work—and how sex with a new lover was always a gamble, and that hopefully, this one would pay off in pleasure, and maybe a new friend.

Jerry joined me with two crystal goblets, and we sat side by side, sipping the cold, dry wine while exchanging meaningful glances in anticipation of what was to come. He surprised me by asking, would he be my first black lover? I said yes, as it happened he was and why did he want to know?

"Curious," he said. "Some white chicks really dig black men. Haven't you heard the saying "Try black, you'll never go back?"

"Sounds catchy to me," I said, smiling, "But it's that *other* rumor that intrigues me."

"You mean the one saying that all us black men are hung like horses?" he asked grinning.

"That's the one," I purred, staring at the bulge under his slacks. I'd already sized him up, if you'll pardon the expression, and knew he'd be well endowed.

"Yeah, baby," he said, nodding his head, "I've heard that there rumor." And with a look that promised I wouldn't be disappointed, he stood up, took my hand, and led me to the spacious bedroom—and the giant, satin covered bed.

I stood near the bed. My heart was racing. Currents of excitement coursed through me as Jerry removed my clothing, piece by piece, in a lazy striptease. He smiled when I was naked, looking me over in a proprietary way that enhanced my excitement. Then he bent to kiss me, with his full lips on mine and his hot tongue exploring my open mouth. I responded eagerly. We kissed for a long time, my breasts pressed deliciously against his chest, until I felt my legs give way beneath me as I dropped to my knees before him, smiling up into his eyes.

Rumor or not, his cock was enormous. It was the color of rich dark chocolate and felt hot and silky smooth in my hands. Feeling high on arousal, I breathed in his sharp, musky scent and stroked it lightly, teasing, tantalizing, before getting down to the business at hand. Spurred on by his moans of excitement, I showed off my skills by deep-throating him with an ease born of practice, in a way that Jake assured me made a man lose his mind.

Pornstars had nothing on me once I got a rhythm going. Linda Lovelace, shove over.

Then it was my turn. On the bed, lying back against the pillows, I felt the mattress move beneath his weight as he sat down beside me, sliding a hand between my legs, and murmuring, "Baby, you are *so hot!*"

He explored my wetness, teasing and caressing with sensitive fingers. The exquisite sensations intensified when he bent to go down on me.

This man understands women, I thought happily, when he allowed me to guide him to where it felt the best. "There, exactly there" I gasped, and a man among men, he stayed exactly there. My excitement mounted and surrendering to his expertise, I exploded into orgasm.

When my breathing returned to normal, I was ready for more. Jerry entered me then, and my hips rose up to meet him. I felt my entire body come alive with sensation and wrapping my legs around his waist, I hung on for the ride.

I almost, but didn't quite climax again, but no matter, I lay beside him afterward, relaxed and feeling fine.

"I'll be here at the Hyatt for most of the summer," Jerry said. We were dressed again and side by side on the plush gray sofa, exchanging smiles—chatting and laughing like old friends in the small hours of the morning, devouring the scrambled eggs, toast, and strong hot coffee delivered by room service.

"Will I see you again, Dorothy?" he asked and smiled, with that cocky, confident look a man gets when he knows he's satisfied his woman.

"You can bet on it," I said, turning to kiss him lightly. "Any man I can laugh with *and* come with is a big-time winner to me."

"I keep it light, baby. That's my style. Just so you know." He placed no special emphasis on the words. He was simply informing me.

"Baby, Don't Get Hooked on Me," I said, quoting the title of the Mac Davis song. "Well, that's

my style too, sweetheart. I couldn't have put that better myself."

We regarded each other for a minute before I turned to the door. I wondered, briefly, aside from the bits of information he'd offered, just who this man was and what events he'd lived through that had shaped the life he lived now. His protective arm went around me as we walked to my car.

"See you soon, baby," he promised, and I knew that I would.

Another perfect relationship had begun.

Perfect Stranger Encounter #8

Alan

Alan was an Aries, high-energy, hot-blooded, proud, super-masculine, and not at all subtle. *What a hunk*, I thought, when we met. Think Marlon Brando in ebony and you've got the picture. He was somewhere in his thirties, medium height, and broad-shouldered, with thick, muscular arms, a tight round ass and an enormous Afro that sprang from his scalp like a nest of curled wires.

Originally from the east coast, he lived in a Spartan, one-bedroom flat in the foggy Outer Sunset, and worked part-time as a bartender while taking classes at City College. Jake said he was saving for a life-changing move to Amsterdam, where he felt people of color were treated with the respect they were due. When Jake told me the guy was *everything* I'd been seeking in a hot lover and *super skilled* at eating pussy, I was immediately intrigued.

On our first date, Alan escorted me to a lecture on African American roots: Racial Injustice in a Racist

Society, delivered by a scholarly looking man in his fifties. The event was held in a shabby storefront in the Lower Haight Ashbury. The audience of about thirty-five people was mostly black, with a sprinkling of white here and there in the room. The talk was inflammatory. An undercurrent of anger was palpable in the room—and although I was in complete agreement with the goals of the civil rights movement, I was bored almost to sleep by the time the lecture ended, and we moved on to the social part of the evening.

"Hey, bro, what's happening? Hey, bro, what's happening? Hey, bro, what's happening?" asked almost everyone, by way of greeting, and with the appropriate black-brother handshake, my date, "Hey, bro'd" them back. He kept a possessive arm around me when he wasn't shaking hands. I got some curious looks, not all of them approving and civil rights movement or not, I felt very white. It was December 1976, after all—Utopia was a long way away.

Later, over drinks at his favorite bar at Haight and Fillmore, Alan filled me in on the countless injustices perpetrated against African Americans in our society.

While Alan waxed eloquent about the sins of prejudice, my mind traveled back to my childhood in the 1950s, when the Isaksons, the wealthiest family in our suburban neighborhood, employed a black nanny named Harriet to care for their young son Vince. Sometimes, on hot summer days, my mom and I joined them at a nearby brook to cool off in the water. Vince and I played happily together, splashing and shrieking. My mom, who didn't swim, sat on a stump on the bank of the brook chatting with Harriet about health, a topic of mutual interest. One day, two big boys with sneering faces rushed up to us, and for reasons I didn't understand then, called Harriet a word I'd never heard before and then pelted her with ripe red tomatoes.

I don't remember what Vince and I said, or what we did when that happened, or Harriet either. I can't say if she stood frozen with shock at the attack, or if she showed anger or fear or outrage at her mistreatment. But what I do remember clearly, so many years later, is my polite, timid mother's exclamation of disgust—before she stepped, deliberately, between the nanny and the tomatoes.

My mom taught me an unforgettable lesson about tolerance and respect that day. I could still see the blotchy stains on Harriet's starched white uniform and on my mother's white arm.

I grew impatient with Alan as he droned on and on. I was, in the interest of experiencing lovers of all colors and creeds, willing to suck his cock, but didn't dig having the entire black cultural struggle shoved down my throat along with it. He finally caught on that I was bored and invited me to his place to get it on. *Here we go*, I thought, *the evening's shaping up.*

Turns out, I was wrong; getting it on only made things worse. This man, it turned out, was more involved in the myth of black man as super-stud, than any white woman I knew.

"I understand you have an exploratory relationship with Jake," he said. "Based on your difficulties reaching orgasm." We were seated on an ancient blue sofa in his austerely furnished living room. The bookcases and walls were dark and darker shades of reddish-brown. There wasn't a plant in the place. His tone was polite, but I caught the hint of a leer behind his smile.

"Why doesn't Jake announce my sexual problems over the radio?" I said, snidely. "Think of all the people he could inform at once."

"I'll consider you a challenge then," Alan said.

Should any woman ask me, I'd tell her to *never, ever* have sex with any man, regardless of race, income level, or religious preference—who wishes to stoke his ego as a lover, using your body to accomplish this. Warning: he'll screw you *half to death,* if necessary, to prove he's a man who can make any woman come. Trust me; I gained this bit of wisdom the hard way—the way most bits of wisdom are gained.

By now I felt ambivalent about having sex with his man, but lured by Jake's promise of great oral sex, I allowed him to take my hand and lead me to his bedroom. Staring possessively, he undressed me with a confident smile. He kissed my mouth and neck and breasts and belly, working his way down to my aroused opening. My eyes were closed taking in the pleasure he offered. *Lots* of pleasure, I couldn't help but notice. Abrasive as he was, he seemed to know precisely how to turn my body on. I wondered if Jake had given written instructions.

The man found my clit with no trouble at all and stayed on it, licking and sucking, maintaining the steady rhythm that works best for me. My breath came in gasps and I moaned with pleasure as my orgasm built, my body arched up, my head fell back and I climaxed mightily.

Still panting, I gazed at Alan thinking how odd that someone so unlikable could be so damned enjoyable in bed.

The problem was since his intention was to prove his prowess, he continued oral sex intending to make me come again. "Wait," I whispered, "let me rest a bit," but he must have thought I didn't mean it because he continued until my female parts went numb and I pushed his head away. He got the message then and climbed onto me for the main feature of the evening—sexual acrobatics, designed to impress and amaze.

The man's cock was sizable and his stamina, frankly, was beyond belief. He went on and on for what seemed like hours, assuring me all the while not to worry, that he wouldn't stop until I came. By this time I no longer cared about having another orgasm of any kind. I was exhausted, my vagina was sore and all I wanted was to go home to my kids where I belonged.

"You didn't come, did you?" It was an accusation.

No, I didn't, I thought. *I willfully and with malice aforethought, kept my orgasm at bay just to thwart you!* I didn't say that aloud. Even worse, I almost lied to spare his feelings, like I'd done with Paul but caught myself in time. "I came when you went down on me, but not while you were in me."

Being truthful with this man wasn't at all like being truthful with Jake—who paid close attention to the nature of my turn-ons, but never judged. Waves of disapproval emanated from Alan—who appeared to take my not having achieved a vaginal orgasm as a personal affront to his manhood.

Flustered by the turn the evening had taken, I got up, preparing to go while Alan sat on his bed and glared at me in silence. His tight-lipped expression was reflected in the mirror above his cheap, painted dresser. As was the oversized poster of Malcolm X giving the black power salute. I was almost dressed when he informed me that my difficulty reaching a vaginal orgasm from penetrative sex stemmed from a refusal to give up control.

Wow, this perfect stranger—growing more *imperfect* by the minute—was pushing my buttons and making me mad. "If I'd wanted to be controlled," I said, coldly, "I would have stayed married."

"You're too wrapped up in being a liberated woman," Alan said, frowning.

"Maybe," I said, tightly. "Like you're wrapped up in being black!"

"I don't believe you have an adequate

conception of what it means to be an African American in our country." He spoke with grave dignity.

I turned to him. "I'm a woman, for crying out loud! Women are discriminated against all over the world—*veiled, cloistered, controlled, and treated as nothing more than male property.* And in this democratic country for Christ's sake, we didn't get to vote until 1920! And female workers earn less for doing the same work as a man. Do you have an adequate conception of that?" I paused, breathing deeply, regarding myself in amazement. I'd never told a man off before without becoming emotionally unglued. Good for me!

"Now listen, I know there's a big mess of injustices between your race and mine," I continued, "but if you ask me, the real problem is that most human beings don't know how to treat each other with respect and compassion. It's a damned shame!"

The man glowered. I was dressed now and at the door. "Take care," I said, and as the door to his apartment closed behind me, Alan became part of my past.

CHAPTER EIGHT

I was moving through men like wildfire through a field of weeds, unwilling to pass up any fantasy, however small, that might be safely acted out in the name of liberation. Still, some of the stranger types I met up with were beginning to get to me.

Heading up the stranger-type-of-stranger department last month had to be Walter, airline pilot, and clean freak. No wonder he didn't complain, as did so many of my lovers, about my requesting he use a condom.

How was I to know? He didn't seem weirder than anyone else. He was my age, thirty-three, medium height and good looking in a clean-cut Robert Redford kind of way. We met at the Japanese Tea Garden one sunny afternoon, where we sipped green tea and chatted while gazing out at the gardens and lovely curved bridge. Later in the evening, after heading home to get the boys started on homework and to cook their dinner, I met up with him again at a restaurant, where he treated me to sushi—after which we went to his place for dessert.

Walter lived alone in a huge, one bedroom flat in the Richmond, in a restored Victorian with built-in bookcases and bay windows that overlooked Golden

Gate Park. Everything in the place was perfect and expensive. The lush, thick carpet was dazzling white. We sat side by side on his antique sofa in front of a fireplace large enough to heat the state of Rhode Island, while sipping Chardonnay from crystal goblets.

If this guy can bring me to orgasm, I thought, we might just have something here.

About then, Walter set down his goblet, gave me a long, deep look and took me into his arms and kissed me—and then, shades of Rhett Butler—swept me into his arms, carried me to bed, stripped off my clothes and after rolling on a condom, proceeded to have sex with me. Not bad, I decided later, beside him in bed, in the afterglow of orgasm brought about by the man's remarkably talented hands. Feeling friendly, I turned to cuddle up to him, but he wasn't there.

"Excuse me," he said, politely, having leaped from the bed and rushed to the bathroom, where he showered, washed his hair, brushed his teeth and emerged dressed in a complete change of clothes.

What have we here? A neurosis I haven't run into so far? "Do you, um, do this whenever you have sex?" I inquired. "I mean, it *is* one in the morning."

"A small idiosyncrasy," he said, avoiding my eyes.

Small idiosyncrasy, indeed. Perhaps this explains why he didn't go down on me.

Walter brewed coffee while I dressed and we sat back down on the sofa, sipping and talking. Fifteen minutes later he set his cup down on the coffee table, gave me a long deep look, then kissed me, swept me up in his arms, carried me to bed and proceeded to initiate sex, again.

Will he do it again I wondered? Stay tuned for the next exciting episode to find out.

"Excuse me," he said the instant we'd finished. Then he leaped off the bed, and dashed for the bathroom.

"Out, out, damned spot! Will no amount of washing cleanse the sin from those soiled little hands?" I paraphrased aloud, chuckling to myself as I pulled on my pants. I wondered if we had sex a third time, would he do it again, but decided that enough was, after all, enough. I was fully dressed when he returned, freshly sterilized and wearing clean clothes, again.

And I thought I had hang-ups!

"Good night. It's been...extraordinary. Don't call me, I'll call you," I said, making my escape. Then once again I was out into the night and on my way home.

The orthopedic surgeon from Mexico City was pretty strange too. I met him at the café and we got to talking. Since his divorce three years ago, his soul cried out for a meaningful relationship. In pursuit of this, he'd taken every class, encounter group and relationship seminar in the Bay Area. Now I thought this might mean he was *aware, grounded,* and *together,* the holy bywords of our age but instead he revealed that he had a proclivity.

I wonder if this guy's proclivity will be stranger

*than the last guy's idiosyncrasy. My friend, Clear,
warned me doctors were a kinky bunch. Okay,
sweetheart, I'm ready; name your proclivity!*

"I want to be intimate with you," he said,
blushing.

"Yes?" I said.

"My fantasy is that we slowly undress each
other." He paused, as though he found it difficult to get
the words out.

"Yes?" I said, kindly. *Come on, out with it.
Don't keep me in suspense.*

"Beneath these," he indicated his designer jeans,
"I'm wearing nylon pantyhose with an opening in front.
Having sex while wearing them is the only way I can
get hard."

"It is, eh?" I nodded gently, envisioning his
smallish cock and balls protruding from the opening.
Moved by the deep desire for acceptance in his eyes, I
agreed to the encounter but the experience was clearly
better for him than it was for me. I didn't see him again.

Just when I thought I'd seen it all, I met Milton,
who was tall, dark and resembled Omar Sharif—and
kept a lifetime supply of Herbal Fresh douche in his
bathroom so he could enjoy oral sex without ever
smelling a woman. He referred to this as 'his little
peculiarity.'

"Well, he was so gorgeous I could hardly
breathe when I looked at him," I confided to Jake the
next day. "So, I compromised my principles and gave it
a go. What a mistake. There I was with Herbal Fresh in

my vagina—having earned, I'm sure, the undying hatred of the entire Women's Liberation Movement— and for what? That man went down on me with the same degree of reservation and thinly disguised distaste I demonstrate when I eat okra. It was so sad. I might in time forgive myself, but Betty Friedan and Gloria Steinem would spit in my eye!"

"Idiosyncrasies, proclivities and peculiarities; *oh my*," I complained to my friends. "Not to mention laziness, selfishness, and general ineptitude!"

"General ineptitude," Clear said. "I think I've dated his brother."

"He has many brothers." Harmony informed us. "They're the ones with the nine fatal flaws, the nineteen major league hang-ups, and a sad inability to discover the true location of my clitoris. And if I assert myself with one of them and ask for what I want in bed, he usually tells me I'm overly aggressive and have ruined the whole encounter."

She and Clear almost collapsed laughing at this bit of humor, but at that moment, I was too annoyed to join in. "And here I thought *I* was the one with hang-ups because I didn't turn on like a water faucet every time a man stuck it in!"

"We all used to think that," Harmony said, "it's part of our female heritage."

"Well, I know better now," I said, "And from now on, I'm playing only with the best. Honey, there are going to be some changes made in this game."

In the interest of upgrading my sex life, I began taking inventory of my current lovers to determine who most deserved me. With careful Virgo attentiveness to method and order, I sorted through the crowd for men among men, mentally setting them in neat piles to keep, or discard. My criteria for keeping a boyfriend at that point in my life was relatively uncomplicated. He had to be interesting. He had to be socially acceptable enough to introduce to my sons. *He had to be able to make me come—at least manually or orally.*

The last two items on the list eliminated the majority of the men I knew.

Of course, I kept Jake. No question there. "You simply don't cut loose a man of a thousand sexual fantasies, even if he is mad as a hatter," I wrote to Carla. "There is a great deal to be said for waking up smiling."

I kept Steve, too. Allison wasn't crazy about him these days, but I felt he had his good points. He was imaginative and quick-witted, with a zany sense of humor and was always good for an in-depth discussion on the human condition, or the price of good pot. I liked him, too, for some Aquarian mystery I was determined to unravel—as well as for certain complex maneuvers he did with his tongue.

Joel, the hippie artist, got the thumbs-up sign, too. I found in him an oddly pleasing mixture of tender romance and total absurdity. Like the time we had sex in a dense patch of woods—a romantic pit-stop on the way to a hot spring—and when I saw him a week later, he had poison oak on his elbows. Or when he cooked me late suppers that he served by candlelight in his ancient claw-footed Victorian bathtub, while we watched *Mary Hartman, Mary Hartman*, his favorite TV show. He eventually became so involved with *Mary* that our dating activities were planned around her nightly, eleven pm show. One evening we mismanaged our time and were still having sex when she came on the air. "Oh, oh," Joel said, and with cock control rare to Western man—he held his erection firm inside me until *Mary* went off the air and thrusting was resumed. Yes, I decided, I liked him. He was cool, creative, entertaining, both of my sons liked him and I came easily under his knowing tongue. He was in like Flynn.

Richard was my elegant, sad-eyed lover—the poet with the big beautiful cock, who wrote poignant love poems to a lost generation that he claimed had forgotten how to love. Honestly, I found him depressing, but then it was his sexual skills I was involved with and they were a blast. I planned to keep him around too.

Jerry, the gambler, was a must in any group. He was in and out of the money, in and out of town, and in and out of me—an odds-on-favorite as far as I was concerned.

I met Curt, an instant add-on, at a party, while in the process of keeping and discarding. He was my first younger man. I'd meant to try one. Clear, Harmony, and Allison all assured me I hadn't lived until I had.

"Younger men aren't cynical, or jaded," they said, "plus they're trainable, tireless, and eager to please."

Curt was a twenty-three-year-old Libra romantic who looked young for his age. "Are you sure that guy's older than me?" This was my son, Brad, the humorist, asking.

"He shaves," I said, "almost every day."

Curt had recently split with his old lady of four years. He told me their sex life had been dull and frustrating. As a man of the 70s, he felt pressured to arouse her to orgasm. And Amy, his ex, came to hate sex because she couldn't have orgasms, or so they thought. Now she'd left him for an older man who was apparently supplying her with those missing orgasms and with whom she now claimed to be in love.

He was heartbroken, lonely, eyed me hopefully, and I rose to the occasion. He was, for the record, trainable, tireless, and eager to please. "Far out," he said, after our first time together, "I've never been with an older woman before.

An older woman at thirty-three

Well, here's to you, Mrs. Robinson. Indeed.

When I finished taking inventory I was weary but *so* pleased with myself—another fantasy had unfolded before my eyes. "Six steady boyfriends? Are you planning to hand out appointment cards?" Clear inquired, eyebrows raised. It was late in the evening and the kids were asleep. She sat cross-legged on the chair near the window, smoking a joint. I was on the sofa sipping tea. We looked at each other and laughed.

"Appointment cards, now that's a thought," I said, straight-faced. "I could assign each man a day of the week. Of course, I won't see each of them weekly. Men are such undependable creatures, after all, and not always around when you want them. But with a group of six, I'm thinking it should average out to about three dates a week—and every one a for sure orgasm. And if one man can't fill my needs, I thought, well, maybe six of them can."

"Dorothy. I love it." Clear wrapped her arms around me and hugged. "You've taken the ultimate male fantasy and reversed it. You now have yourself a male harem."

"Yes, like a gaggle of geese."

"A what?"

"A gaggle of geese," I explained, laughing, "A gaggle of geese; a stable of studs."

Dear Carla,

Happy 1977! It's been more than a year since we've seen each other, and well over two since I divorced Paul. I've been through some heavy changes since then. I wonder when we meet again if you'll recognize your shy, frightened, little friend. Might not you know; she doesn't exist anymore—at least as far as the untrained eye can see. I'm wiser and stronger these days—coming into my own, at last, and with my battered ego flying high!

I'm pleased to report that I'm soaking in male attention these days, like a plant that's spent years living in the darkest of corners would soak up the sun. I feel desirable, sought after, and damn proud of having the balls to take control of my love life. The stud stable I mentioned in my recent letter takes care of the orgasm situation quite nicely—and keeps the loneliness at bay. For now, I'm quite satisfied. Five talented men, plus Jake, are keeping me delightfully entertained; each man in his own distinct style. What fun.

Having a man for my every mood has its illuminating moments. For instance, I become a different woman with each one, observing with fascination the various aspects of my personality that emerge from within me and try themselves on for size.

I become an assertive, but tender, Mrs.

Robinson with my sweet young thing, Curt and walk a mile in Jake's shoes, as I take Curt on journeys into *his* secret fantasies—while with Jake I revert back to the novice in training, allowing him to lead me into his world of sex and sensation.

I'm a stable respite from an unawakened world for my pal, Steve; a fun-loving swinging single with Jerry, the gambler; and a sensual, funny playmate with Joel. To my surprise, I'm a bit of a bitch with Richard—arriving at his place late in the evening after the kids are asleep, demanding to be royally pleasured.

In some crazy way, Carla, even though I haven't touched clay in a long time, I feel that I am sculpting after all—only for right now, the object I'm molding is me. Will the real Dorothy Freed please stand up?

Sure thing; as soon as I've figured out *who* the real Dorothy Freed is.

My women friends, who are all lonely right now, envy me my popularity. "How do you do it?" they ask. "How do you keep them eager and excited and coming back for more, and hassle-free in the bargain?"

I shrug in response and say, with a grin, "I'm easy to get along with. I don't cling or ask for commitments—and I put out big time. They keep coming back because I accept them for who they are in the little private world we share together—and ask nothing of them but pleasure."

So that's life on the funny farm these days: *"Curiouser and Curiouser,"* as Alice so wisely said.

And it beats being married, as far as I can see.

Marriage to me meant always having to say I'm sorry. A stable of studs means always having a good time—without the hassle of a husband raining on my parade with *his* version of how I should be and how life should be lived.

Write soon. Tell me what's happening in your world. Are you still enjoying life in suburbia, and more importantly are you still enjoying life with Ray?

The kids send hellos to your boys and their other friends in the neighborhood. Doug said to tell you that he had a lead part in his school play and is now considering a future acting career.

Brad, the teenager, has no idea what he wants to do when he grows up, but right now his favorite classes are music and art, and he's excellent at both. He's all excited about taking a girl to a school dance next week for the first time. I'll let you know how that goes.

I've enclosed photos of the boys on the new banana seat bikes I bought them for Christmas. Brad's was stolen almost immediately after, but he spotted it in front of a neighborhood store—complete with certain identifying marks he'd made on it—and stole it back. Such is life in the big city.

I miss you. Take care. Write soon.

Love,
Dorothy

P.S.—My mom's threatening a two-week visit during the kid's summer vacation. They'll be overjoyed to see her. I guess I will too, but she's always a downer since she never let's go of the past. Sigh.

Perfect Strangers

CHAPTER NINE

For the next few months, I played around happily. No two ways about it, I was having a ball. There were parties, art galleries, and drives in the country. There were ethnic restaurants, hot tubs, and listening to live music. There was a *lot* of sex.

The attention I got did wonders for my confidence. Each time I had sex I felt myself relax more deeply into the pleasure of it. One by one I felt my remaining inhibitions sigh and give up the ghost.

Vaginal orgasm was but a heartbeat away.

I experienced it with Jake—as was only fitting—one stormy night on my bedroom rug after the kids were asleep. I'm certain Jake planned the whole thing. He gave me some particularly intense looks as he moved about the room, setting the stage for a passionate encounter. Lamps were switched off and replaced by candlelight. The smell of sandalwood drifted from a stick of incense in a jar on the window ledge. We lay naked on the bed, side by side with our heads propped up on pillows, smoking grass from Jake's small glass pipe. The sound of rain spattering against the windows merged with the Indian sitar music coming from the stereo and filled the room.

Jake was talking as we lay there, expounding in his enthusiastic way, on some new theory about female sexual response that had occurred to him, but I was drifting through some private inner space and only half-listening. The exciting sounds around me combined with the exotic smell of the incense and the quality of the grass. I was acutely conscious of the steady hum of arousal in my lower belly, and of the involuntary clenching of my inner muscles and cheeks of my ass. Excitement coursed through me. I felt turned on and lit up from the inside out. When Jake turned and reached for me, I melted into his arms, responding to his seeking hands and mouth, and the scorching heat of his skin.

Inspired by my enthusiasm, Jake performed an entire medley of my favorite moves from our past times together; teasing, tormenting, and delighting me until I was writhing on the bed, dripping wet, back arching, head thrown back, and panting to be taken.

But Jake, luxuriating in his power to bring me to this state, proceeded at his own pace, making me wait, teasing my swollen labia with the head of his cock and making my clit pulse with need. Finally, he took me, thrusting himself deep and deeper inside me, with his knowing cock probing my most sensitive places. He kissed my mouth, my ears, my neck, and the furry ness of his chest crushed against my aching nuckered nipples. Moaning, I wrapped my legs around him, and my hips rose up to meet his thrust as I hung on for the ride.

I don't remember how we ended up on the floor, with Jake on top, plunging and withdrawing, grinding the base of his cock against my clit, again and again. He continued on until 1 was floating in a sea of sensation—gasping for breath as my entire body tensed and my excitement mounted. "Reach down and play with your clit," he whispered hoarsely, guiding my hand.

I did as he said, and the place between my legs felt like molten lava. My entire body was tingling and flushed with heat. In my head I envisioned white-hot light, bubbling up and radiating out in ever-widening rings that enveloped me. And surprise, surprise, in the missionary position no less—my body stiffened, my toes curled, and I came with a man's cock inside me, for the first time in my life!

"You came while I fucked you, am I right?" Jake asked when we'd finished. He knew already though, I could tell by the gleam of triumph in his eyes.

I was still bathed in afterglow and felt incapable of speech, but nodded and smiled at him, sharing the moment of triumph with him—even as I analyzed in my head any existing differences between a vaginal orgasm and a clitoral one.

Clitoral alone might be more intense, I thoug It's all about me and without distractions, whe vaginal is obviously more of a shared experienc wait a minute, I was rubbing my clit when I came during intercourse—so did that make it vaginal or clitoral? And how about when I've come before with a dildo inside me and a vibrator on my clit—which kind of orgasm would that be?

Who knows and who gives a damn! I decided, finally. The *real* myth of the vaginal orgasm has got to be the assertion that it matters in any way how an orgasm comes about. All orgasms are heaven-on-earth as far as I'm concerned. I can't imagine what difference it could possibly make to anyone, which kind a woman has—as long as she's lucky enough to have them.

Still, I'd waited a long time for this moment and was delighted with this new dimension to my sex life. "We did it!" I exulted. "I came during sexual intercourse!" I told Jake. "And it appears I was misinformed. I'm not frigid at all. Turns out what it took to make me a hot woman was exploration, trust, and letting sex be fun."

What do you think about that Paul, you son-of-a-bitch?

ow what I thought would happen once I'd
nced a vaginal orgasm. I think I expected
bles would melt away—*like lemon
the chimney tops*—and that from
 my way through a perfectly
, if there is such a thing,
n that.

190

For several weeks after that night with Jake, I went wild. Impressed all to hell with my new-found ability, I had more sex than ever and managed a few more orgasms during intercourse. Perfect, I thought. Still, since my life was such a whirlwind of activity, I was too exhausted most of the time to acknowledge the small voice in my head informing me that something was still missing from my life. The problem was, despite all my efforts to prevent such an occurrence, stud stable or not, I found it increasingly difficult to keep myself amused.

Concerned with this serious state of affairs, I shopped around for an addition to the stable, to bring in new energy and keep things lively. I came up with Arthur, a Capricorn art gallery owner. A "silver fox" of fifty-two, with a Master's degree in Art History and an excellent imagination. Together we gallery hopped, dined in fine restaurants, spent an evening at the opera and another at the ballet. He added a bit of glamour to my motley crew.

But still, that voice in my head whispered, plaintively—*something's wrong, Dorothy, something's missing from your life… Uh-oh*, I thought, *there's trouble in paradise.*

Perfect Strangers

CHAPTER TEN

As I recall, my perfect little bubble began to burst one sunny spring morning when, after seeing the boys off to school, rather than enjoying the temporary peace and quiet in my apartment, I felt suddenly and unbearably alone. Shrinking from the uncomfortable feeling, I thought ahead to my evening's entertainment. *With whom shall I fool around?* I wondered. *Who's out there for adventure; for self-developmental experience? For a bit of fine madness and a primo lay?*

I ran my men through my mind and couldn't think of anyone I wanted.

Something's changed. Could it be me? The thought alarmed me, and I pushed it away. But my mood persisted, and by evening I'd spoken to and turned down the company of most of my stable. Faithful as ever, they began calling in the late afternoon.

"Mom, it's for you," Doug yelled. "It's that tall bummed-out looking guy."

It was Richard. He'd written two new poems and man was he depressed from the deep underlying truth of his words. Would I like to come by for a reading, or anything else he could offer me? Not tonight, I decided, although I loved the stimulation of his quick, bright mind—not to mention other parts. "Soon though,

193

sweetheart," I said.

"It's that snobby guy," Brad told me in a loud whisper a few minutes later. "You know who I mean; the one who pretends to like kids so he can get in good with you, Mom." *Out of the mouths of babes*, I thought and took the phone.

Arthur invited me to a private function at the San Francisco Museum of Modern Art. Some well-off collectors would be there. He expected to make important business connections and get us to his elegant Sacramento Street flat by ten-thirty, with ample time for sex. Exciting as that sounded, I wasn't in the mood. "Sweetheart, I'm so sorry, I'm just not into it tonight. Have a great time connecting and call me soon."

When the phone rang again, it was Jerry, who'd just arrived in town. Pretty Princess would run a stakes race the next day at noon. How would I feel about tripping on out to his hotel for dinner and some heavy love, to put him in a winning rhythm? The man was delightful, I decided, and highly entertaining, but not what I wanted that night. "Thanks for asking, love, but I'll take a rain check," I said.

Joel shyly offered to show me his latest painting and to draw me a bath. "Had one for lunch, baby," I told him. "Talk to you soon."

Curt, my youngest lover, invited me out to smoke grass, listen to some far out live music and just hang out. "Sorry, baby, we'll do it another time for sure, but not tonight."

Steve didn't call. An irregular regular, he turned

up now and then, offering New Age wisdom, good sex and some mystery of Aquarian maleness I sought to unravel in his veiled and unreadable eyes.

"Hello, sweetheart," rasped the voice on the phone in a horror movie whisper. "I'm going to fuck you, but first, I'm going to stick four fingers up your cunt and pinch your nipples—not hard enough to hurt, but hard enough so you'll know you're being pinched. Then I'll bend you over a table and make you lay there waiting for me to stick my throbbing cock deep inside your hot, dripping wet cunt..." The voice broke off. There was the sound of heavy breathing.

"Hi Jake," I said, "An obscene phone call; thanks, sweetheart, that's just what I wanted."

"That's what I'm for, to give you what you want," he said, agreeably. "Listen, sweetheart, here's what I want you to do tonight. Put on something sexy with a long skirt and *nothing* underneath it. I want to take you somewhere sleazy."

"Jake, I don't know what's gotten into me tonight, but I just don't feel sleazy."

So my men checked in and I wasn't in the mood for them. I took the kids out for Chinese food, followed by *The Night of the Living Dead* at the Balboa Theater. I bought a huge tub of popcorn, dripping with butter and sat between my sons with the tub in my lap. We gobbled it up. I thought the film was completely gross, with gore galore, but both Brad and Doug enjoyed every minute of it. We three had a wonderful time.

I wish, I thought later, *there was a man I could be real with, like I'm real with my kids. Where is there a man who will see me—not the sexy, independent persona I present to him?*

"See me, Feel me, Touch me..." I whispered The Who's haunting lyrics softly under my breath. I was happy to be home with my sons, Brad and Doug, who knew and loved me.

"Mom, you wouldn't exactly be my type if I was a grown-up, but in your own way, you're really beautiful." This was Doug, perfectly illustrating the art of the left-handed compliment as he bear-hugged me goodnight. I hugged him back fiercely.

To his surprise and mine, I realized I was crying.

Perfect Stranger Encounter #9

Stuart

Stuart called early the next morning while I was still in bed. He'd been out of town, alone on his motorcycle exploring Nevada and Southern Utah, and then on to Arizona to meet up with some friends. No timetable. Be back whenever. I hadn't seen him in more than two months.

"Hello, sweetheart," he said. "Can I talk you into joining me for breakfast?"

Funny, he always said, "Hello, sweetheart," and Jake did too and didn't they sound different? Sleepy, I forced an eye open and fought for coherency. "Stuart it's early morning..."

"That's why I want breakfast," he said in his low, soothing voice.

Suddenly, I felt happy. I had a lot on my mind. It would feel good to share it with someone who'd understand. "What time is it?" I asked. "How soon are you coming? Where have you been?"

"Be there in an hour. I'll talk while you get

ready. I want to tell you about Bryce Canyon, Utah, and Jerome, Arizona."

I put down the phone and bumbled around getting organized. Stuart arrived as I was shooing the boys out the door toward school.

"Stuart!" Doug yelled and leaped at him. Stuart caught him and lifted him over his head.

"Put me down! Put me down!" Doug shouted, but I could tell the attention delighted him.

"Will you take us for a bike-ride?" Brad asked.

"I came to take your mom for a ride right now, but how about later today? I'll be here then, if I can talk your mom into dinner and the movies."

"Say yes, Mom! Dinner! Movie! Motorcycle ride! Say yes, Mom!" the kids chorused.

"How can I say no?" I asked, pretending to complain. But I didn't mind at all.

I felt completely safe seated behind Stuart on the motorcycle. His back was so broad I was sheltered from the wind as we rode west toward the ocean. By the time we were seated in the Cliff House restaurant watching the waves crashing against Seal Rock below, I felt more relaxed than I had in a long time.

"Once, near the New Mexico border, I rode all night," Stuart said. "I was blind tired, but couldn't make myself stop moving. I remember thinking that the way I felt that night must be how birds feel when they fly, free."

His imagery stirred something inside me, bringing Nina Simone's song lyrics to my head. "*I Wish I Knew How It Would Feel To Be Free*," I said, softly. My voice trailed off. "I've never been free, Stuart. Not like you're talking about." Tears pooled in my eyes. Selecting a slice of sourdough bread, I buttered it carefully to cover my confusion. I blinked back the tears, but Stuart saw them. Somehow it wasn't a big deal.

"I went from my parents' house to Paul's house," I said abruptly. "I had Brad when I was eighteen and Doug at twenty-two. While I was married, I never held a job, never took a trip alone. I was officially an adult, but the truth is, except for the years I spent at the university, I never felt like one—and didn't until I was thirty-years-old and driving my kids across country and finally in charge of myself."

I fell silent, remembering my life with Paul. Remembering what it felt like to be second in command. A grown-up person with no income of my own and having to ask for what I wanted or needed like a child: clothing, art supplies, and everything else. It was Paul's money after all—he earned it; he controlled it—and Paul's version of how life should be lived. Not to mention his take on how a woman should respond in bed. Remembering brought the usual surge of anger toward my ex-husband and a surprising surge of anger toward myself.

Stuart sipped his coffee and watched me. I wondered if my face reflected my thoughts.

"I have a job now," I said. "And I provide for my family. I feel good about that and I do... what I do with my personal life, and answer only to myself. But still, I've never been free. And I want so much to go *somewhere over that rainbow,* Stuart. I want..." I stopped speaking and picked at the home fries on my plate with my fork, embarrassed by my intensity. Men weren't into hearing this heavy stuff.

"I'm sorry," I said, shaking my head and throwing up my hands. "You invited me to breakfast and here I am going on and on like a fool."

Stuart's large hand was warm on my cheek. He grinned. "Don't be so hard on yourself, Dorothy. You don't have to decide the rest of your life right now. You had a bad trip with your old man, so give yourself time to get over it. Maybe you'll work with clay again when you're ready. I think you really loved doing that. But for now, you're taking care of your family, and learning about yourself and what you want and need in your life—so, no worries."

The man understands me, I thought, *far out.* Now I was curious about him. "You've been married, haven't you?"

"Twice. I was twenty-two the first time. It lasted all of eight months."

"Why did you split up?"

Stuart laughed and shook his head. "We were so young when we married neither of us had a clue who we were or what we wanted from life. It's hard to know another person if you don't know yourself." He shrugged. "So, we fought a lot, each trying to control the other until we were sick of fighting. Then we got a divorce."

"Anatomy of a marriage," I said in a low voice. "We fought, got sick of fighting, got divorced. What about your second wife? Did you love her?"

"Yes, I loved Carrie a lot." Stuart paused and leaned back in his chair, stretching his long legs under the table as he continued his story.

"I had forty acres of land in Mendocino County. We built our dream house there. Planted a vegetable garden, talked about having kids. We were in love and expected our marriage to last the rest of our lives. But I was a different person then. More harsh than I am now. More into writing my own rules. Turned out I had a natural talent as a pot grower, so I hired some help and grew great pot and made a great living. Carrie and I lived high on the hog for a while."

"So what happened," I asked. "What made it go wrong?"

"One day I got busted selling an ounce of pot to a dude who turned out to be a narc. That put me in state prison for almost a year. I'd have been there longer, but as it happened, Carrie helped get me out—in exchange for a divorce. She'd met someone while I was away—a wealthy, influential man who wanted her. If I let her go, her boyfriend would use his money and influence to get me paroled."

"What a terrible decision to make," I said. "So you did it?"

"Yes, I did." Stuart's voice was calm. "At first I wanted to beg her to wait for me, give me another chance to set things right between us. But when I looked into her eyes, I knew the marriage was over." He smiled. "And above all else, I wanted to be free."

This man, I thought, *doesn't talk much, but when he does, he has a lot to say.* I'd known him for more than a year now, but hadn't seen much of him lately, involved as I was with my many lovers. But I believe he was the first male friend I'd ever had. I felt sure he would have been happy to become my lover, but I didn't respond to his subtle hints, and he never pushed it.

Best to keep it this way—friends are friends, and lovers are lovers. Mixing the two could lead only to grief, I felt sure. The thought saddened me. For the third time in twenty-four hours, I felt tears in my eyes. Looking away to hide my show of emotion, I sipped at the now cold coffee in my cup.

Stuart pretended not to notice. "Finished with breakfast?" His tone was light. I nodded yes, not trusting my voice. He reached for the check. "Then let's get outside and go for a walk."

The wind from the sea dried my tears as we climbed down a sandbank, near the ruins of the old Sutro Baths, a once fashionable resort that burned down years before—no relation to the sex club of the same name that I'd frequented with Jake. Reaching the beach, we stood watching the Pacific Ocean roll in and out in its timeless, unending rhythm. A fine mist of salty seaspray touched my face, settled in my hair and calmed me. I took a long, deep breath and began to relax.

"I'm sorry, Stuart. I wanted to hear about your trip, but I seem to have gotten us off on another subject."

"Tell you what," he deadpanned, "tonight at the movies I'll tell you all about my trip."

"Please don't talk at the movies. I hate when people do that," I kidded back, grateful for his sensitivity to my feelings.

Later we took the kids out for Mexican food and to a horror thriller that had Doug holding my hand the whole time—he'd be crawling into bed with me later that night, I could tell. The boys liked Stuart. They talked and joked with him like he was family.

Later still, after I got them to bed, I made coffee and we sat sipping it in my quiet living room. And all the while I kept thinking of my friend locked in a prison cell—forced, he said, to take the time to come to terms with himself and the life choices he'd made.

In a flash of insight, I realized why he understood me so well. He understood himself.

"Stuart, don't you ever look back on your life and miss it?" I asked. "Not because that life was so great—but because you knew it was set into some sort of secure, predictable pattern?" My voice dropped to a whisper. "I get tired of walking bravely out into the unknown."

"I stopped grieving over the past," he said, "when I realized that hanging on to it interfered with the present. Looks to me like we all walk into the unknown every day we're alive, married or not, happy or not. It's still true."

Restless, I moved to the window and stared out into the night. Stuart got up and stood beside me. "Dorothy," he said, and as I turned to face him, he bent and kissed my lips, taking me by surprise.

I was confused. I didn't know what to do with that kiss. I'd checked out plenty of kisses since Paul was water under the bridge—passionate ones, demanding ones. But my friend Stuart's kiss was gentle and friendly and I had no idea how to deal with that.

"It's late and I have a house to paint tomorrow. Goodnight," he said, and moved toward the door. I stood watching him go, amazed that he asked for nothing from me. No payment, no performance, no promise of anything—just a goodnight kiss from a friend.

"Goodnight, Stuart. Thanks for a great evening." I said and closed the door behind him.

CHAPTER ELEVEN

Jake called the next evening, and I was happy to hear from him, having brooded all day about Stuart and the deep underlying meaning behind the sweetness of his kiss. Jake was just what I needed. I wore a sexy, low-cut dress with nothing beneath it and let him lead me out into the night to where it was sleazy. Feeling wild and free as the wind itself, I followed him, roaming the Land of Oz in search of sensation.

Fun and games that night began with a ride through Golden Gate Park in the moonlight. Jake drove while I gave him a blowjob that lasted from one end of the park to the other. Later we went to the Castro, where we sat out on the sheltered patio at Café Flore on Market Street observing gay men meet and greet, and feeling the vibration of raw sexual energy in the foggy night air. The 'real world' with its cares and worries slipped silently away as I accompanied Jake into his world of sexual fantasy that made me higher than any drug I might have taken.

He was all over the place, strutting around, Marlon Brando style. The epitome of macho in the silver studded, black leather jacket he'd chosen for the occasion. Coolly seductive, he noted admiring glances from interested men. Furtively slipping a hand beneath my skirt, he whispered his plans for when we returned home to my bed.

"You're stark raving mad!" I told him and laughed with delight—while my friend Stuart, whom I suspected had serious intentions toward me, faded into the background and out of sight.

In the midst of my days of fantasies and glory, although I admitted it to no one but Carla, I was still haunted by thoughts of Paul and how our life together had played out. Mostly, I thought of him with loathing; as an irresponsible jerk, who'd turned his own children and me loose in the world to sink or swim, while he most likely lived off Cassandra, who'd promised to nurture his literary talent. But sometimes, when the moon was full and no mad escapade could keep my loneliness at bay, I recalled, as people do, the good times and grieved for what was. I wondered if he was happy with her—and if, together, they'd somehow achieved some perfect, evolved level of partnership of which I still only dreamed.

I thought I'd never know, but life, as the saying goes, is just crammed full of surprises. I found that out when Carla called one brisk spring morning to inform me that Paul had stopped by for a visit. He'd expressed love, regret and longing for his children, and wanted to reconnect.

"He asked me for your address and phone number," she said. "And I asked straight out if he was working and planned to send child support."

My heart was pounding. "What did he say?"

"He said some stuff that didn't make sense about planetary positions on his astrology chart, and the after-effects of some transit though your partnership house."

"Do you think that means he has a job? Can I sue him for child support?"

"I don't know, Dorothy. He's still with Cassandra, you know." She paused, and said gently, "They were married a few months ago and still live in Nevada. He's writing a book on astrology and casting charts here and there. From what he said, I suspect what he earns doing charts is probably cash and off the record. She works in a casino as a blackjack dealer. Paul says she's doing well."

"Maybe I can sue her for child support," I said.

"So, shall I tell him how to find you?"

I thought it over. If I let Paul know where I was, there was at least a chance he might come up with some money. And of course, there were the boys' feelings to consider. Regardless of what I thought of him, Paul was their father. He'd disappointed them, but they continued to love him and would be overjoyed to reconnect with him. I took a deep breath and let it out, slowly. "Yes, tell him how to find me."

"I will, but Dorothy, listen to me. If he shows up in San Francisco, don't let him get to you by bringing up the past and playing the blame game. You've got a new life now. None of that old stuff matters anymore."

No worries, I told her. I was a new woman now, tough and independent. Paul couldn't get to me anymore. But despite my brave talk, when I hung up the phone I realized he had gotten to me already. I had a headache and heartache, and neither one was letting up. That night after the kids were asleep, I went out in search of sexual adventure to ease the pain.

I was apprehensive for the next few weeks, uneasily aware that Paul might be lurking around the next corner—ready and willing to barge right in and disrupt my far-out new life. Finally, I relaxed and decided the whole thing was a false alarm.

Not surprisingly, he showed up almost immediately after that.

Perfect Stranger Encounter #10

Paul

Paul showed up the evening Jake and I attended the opening of Lyle Tuttle's tattoo art exhibition at Fort Mason Art Center. What a great show—on the walls and on the audience. I noticed and admired a tight, multi-colored bolero jacket worn by the Rubenesque redhead across the room. Zooming in for a closer look I saw the woman was wearing a halter top. The rest of the bright flowing colors and images were etched into her skin.

Jake, a true art lover, was particularly taken with a large color photo of an aggressive looking penis and balls—every inch of it tattooed in vivid reds and blues.

"Far fucking out," he said, obviously awed by admiration. "What do you think of *that,* sweetheart? And that yellow sunburst on his pubes, well, that makes the whole thing just right, don't it?" He grinned, lewdly caressing the tattoo on his right forearm—a naked lady, of course, in blues and greens. "How'd you like having *that* cock inside you?"

209

Later, as we climbed the stairs to my apartment, I was still thinking about the brightly colored cock emerging from a yellow sunburst pubis, thrusting its way into me. "Question is would it give a better orgasm?" I asked, as I opened the door to my apartment and stared straight at Paul.

He sat on the sofa with Doug on his lap and Brad beside him. If I hadn't known he was their father, I could have guessed by how the boys, Brad in particular, resembled him. With their light brown hair and eyes, high cheekbones and enigmatic expressions. Brad and Paul bore a striking resemblance to the late actor, James Dean, also an Aquarian, in the film *Rebel without a Cause*. We all stared at each other without speaking. Seeing Paul again set off years of memories that hit me rapid-fire, like bullets from a gun. My breathing became slow and labored and I felt as though a great weight was sitting on my chest.

I looked at Brad, and his eyes met mine. What I saw in them was comprehension beyond his years— along with all the innocent confusion of a child. I stared at Paul as if he was some sort of hallucination while all kinds of conflicting emotions leaped around inside me. I couldn't think of a single thing to say.

Doug broke the silence. "Dad's here," my ten-year-old informed me.

"I should have called," Paul said, "but I didn't know if you'd talk to me, so I just came."

"Would you like some coffee?" I said finally, thinking that I sounded like some damned housewife in a TV commercial, but it was all I could think to say. Paul nodded yes, and shakily, I turned toward the kitchen.

Jake followed close on my heels, jabbering in my ear in a loud whisper. "So that's the old man, huh? How does it feel seeing him, again? Hey, is he a jealous type? I mean he's not going to try to *kill* me or anything like that?"

I gave him a sharp look. He sounded worried. I supposed that to a sexual liberator, husbands and ex-husbands were people to avoid.

"Oh stop worrying," I said irritably. "He's not going to try to kill anyone. And *I don't know* how I feel, if you really want to know. I think you should go and let me deal with this."

"Okay, but let me kiss you goodbye first, sweetheart," he said, taking me into his arms. With a furtive glance toward the living room, he slipped his hand down my jeans and stealthily caressed my ass. I laughed aloud in spite of myself. *A Jake is a Jake is a Jake*, I thought. And there he was getting turned on at the thought of feeling me up in the kitchen with a potentially murderous ex-husband in the next room.

I pried him loose. "Call me tomorrow," I said, kissing him and shooing him out the door. Then I took a deep breath, exhaled slowly and turned my attention to making coffee and arranging chocolate chip cookies on a plate.

Paul and I were nothing if not polite.

"Do you still take milk in your coffee?"

"Please."

"Here you are, and how about a cookie?'

"Thanks."

"You're welcome."

"The boys are so much taller."

"Yes. They've grown."

"You have a nice bright apartment," he said, looking around the room.

"Thanks. "I said. "Would you like another cookie?"

Great dialogue folks, we'll be discussing the weather next. *Did you know it never rains in California? It pours man, it pours.*

Since I still couldn't think of anything to say to this man I'd made babies with and who'd been my husband for twelve years, I sat there and did some non-stop remembering while Brad and Doug chattered away about school and life in the city, and all the new friends they'd made. Then it was late in the evening and the boys went reluctantly to bed with the promise from their dad they'd see him again soon.

And there we were, Paul and I, together again— blown by the tornado of our divorce, from our home, far away, to my living room here in the Land of Oz.

I studied him. There was some subtle difference in the way he looked, but I couldn't put my finger on precisely what that difference was. He'd gained a bit of weight since I'd last seen him and his hair was grayer and worn longer than before. That wasn't it, though. He wore a wedding ring on the fourth finger of his left hand, a bright shiny wedding ring, but that wasn't it either. I eyed him, dispassionately. He was medium height, still reasonably trim and deeply suntanned. Except for his mouth which was tight and angry looking. He *was* a good-looking guy—even if he *was* a prick. But still, wasn't there a time when he was more handsome, more vibrant, and dynamic; taller too? Or had I simply perceived him that way? I couldn't be sure.

"Why did you come, Paul, after all this time?"

"I've missed the kids. I want to arrange for visitation and to be part of their lives again."

"Forgive my material crassness, but does this brave new plan for family togetherness happen to include child support?" I inquired.

"I don't have a job right now," he said, avoiding my eyes. "But I earn a little money these days as an astrological counselor. I'll send what I can when I can and the boys can come to stay with me anytime."

Paul's voice sounded cool and in control, but I saw that his fingers were tap, tap, tapping on the arm of his chair and a tense little muscle jumped in his jaw. *Why, he's more shook up by this visit than I am*, I thought, surprised.

"Well, the kids were happy to see you tonight and now we've promised them they'll see you again," I shrugged. "I guess we'll have to work something out."

There was another silence, then he said, "I wanted to see you too, Dorothy. I went to a lot of trouble to find you."

"I heard. Carla called."

"I suppose it must be hard for you to understand everything that's happened."

I felt a prickle of annoyance. Somehow, he'd managed to convey the impression that any misunderstanding about anything that had passed between us, was mine alone.

"Look, the fact is, we never should have gotten divorced," he said.

"Shouldn't we have?" I snapped. "I can think of at least a dozen excellent reasons myself. By the way, speaking of the best reason of all—where's your wife, my good friend, Cassandra? Surely she's hovering nearby in case you need her?"

Paul looked irritated. "Cassandra wasn't sure if she'd be welcome here," he explained, reasonably. "She's visiting old friends in another neighborhood while I'm visiting here and will pick me up later. You know, Dorothy," he said, with judgment, "you *shouldn't* be so bitter."

Shouldn't be bitter? Why the hell shouldn't I?

Interesting isn't it; old friends push old buttons and old reactions set right in.

"Damn it," I snarled, "I am bitter! For twelve years I tried as hard as I knew how to give you whatever it was you wanted from a woman: I cooked, cleaned, shopped, tried to be a good mom—we had sex whenever you wanted it, however you wanted it. I even faked orgasms to make *you* feel like more of a man—which, by the way, made *me* feel like shit! What *was* it you wanted Paul? I never did figure it out, never got it right. But still, I tried because I thought that's what married people were supposed to do until death did them part. But when you decided you were a New Age person who rated two wives, you asked too much of me!"

Paul gave me a withering look—the one that used to deflate me and put me in my place. He sighed, exasperated. "Look, the cause of our problems is complex. I was bored with my job, felt frustrated and futile. Never got going as a writer. I felt like I couldn't satisfy you, in bed or anywhere else."

"Paul, if you tell me my unpassionate nature was the cause of our problems one more time, I'm going to throw up right here in front of you!"

"Listen, Dorothy," he went on with dignity. "If *you* hadn't over-reacted to an indiscretion on my part and insisted on a divorce, we could have worked things out and gone on with our lives."

"I overreacted?" I repeated, my voice rising four octaves. "Paul, you said you were madly in love with Cassandra! In case this little detail slipped your mind, I found the two of you in bed together!"

"Dorothy, you just don't get it do you?" He sounded pissed off and shook his head, in disbelief, dismayed by my stupidity. "I was in love with both of you, but various astrological influences in 1974 created the additional element of compulsion between Cassandra and me."

This guy's not for real. "Compulsion," I sneered, "do you mean like that book about the murderers, *Leopold and Loeb?*"

Once we got going, even my new life and Paul's remarriage didn't stop us. Bitterness flowed fast and free as we screamed out our disappointments at each other late into the night.

He told me I'd never given him the attention he needed from a woman. His Cancer moon craved emotional security above all, which I had *willfully* refused to provide.

I told him I hated him for making me feel guilty about wanting a career as a professional artist.

He told me how disappointed he was by my inability to come during intercourse—it made him feel like less of a man.

I told him, loudly at that point, that he was an insensitive jerk, for leading me to believe I was a frigid woman—which for his information, I was not!

Yep. It's true. Old friends, old buttons.

"Are you happy with Cassandra, Paul?" I asked finally, when we'd exhausted ourselves and become quiet again. *Tell me,* I thought, gazing into the veiled brown eyes that once held such charm for me. They were cold and guarded and didn't meet mine. *Please, please, tell me your truth whatever it is. I know we don't communicate, have never communicated, and will never communicate—but answer me this one question, because damn it, I need to know!*

"Yes. I'm happy with her," he said without joy. "To her, I matter more than anything."

The doorbell rang. It was Cassandra, right on cue. I hadn't seen her since that agonizing night three years ago. I took an enormous breath, remembering how she'd been my best friend and my husband's lover at the very same time, and gestured stiffly for her to enter my home. Then, I made more coffee and we all sat in the living room and made polite small talk about the kids. She was Brad and Doug's stepmother now. I should be civilized for their sake.

Still, I was pleased to see that her hair was going gray and that she'd put on weight—her butt was the size of a bus.

"Tell the boys I'll be in touch," Paul said when the visit ended. "And here's a number where I can be reached. Have them call me anytime. During the summer we'll arrange to have them visit us. And if you agree, Dorothy, they could visit us during Easter and Christmas vacations too."

"Sure Paul. The boys would like that. We'll work out the dates."

We stood looking at each other for a long drawn out minute. Then he was gone, out the door, riding off into the sunset toward his particular brand of happily ever after, leaving me to discover mine.

Who was that Masked Man? Heigh ho,

Cassandra, away!

CHAPTER TWELVE

I didn't sleep well that night. I had a long, involved dream that Paul and I were locked up together in a tiny room having the same terrible argument over and over. "Let me out! Let me out!" I pleaded, but the door remained closed.

When I woke the next morning, I was alone. Brad had left me a note saying he thought I might need extra sleep, so he'd seen himself and his brother off to school. "I made us breakfast," he'd added. I'd already figured that one out for myself since the entire kitchen was covered with Cheerios and little crumbs of toast.

"Thanks, sweetheart," I said aloud, and smiling, tucked the note away with the baby teeth I kept in a box on a shelf in my closet, along with tiny first pairs of shoes, undershirts with spit-up stains and feather-soft locks of hair—precious memorabilia we moms tend to lug with us wherever we go. *I have a beautiful family*, I thought and my spirits lifted. The three of us are doing fine.

I made coffee and sat sipping it in my sunny kitchen, thinking, with pride that we'd come a long way together on our own. Paul disagreed, I recalled, with a flash of anger. *He* felt San Francisco was no fit place to raise kids. A really good mother would move to a small town or suburb, where the boys wouldn't be exposed to evil influences.

Evil influences, my ass! As far as I was concerned, it was an evil influence for kids to have two parents who were always at each other's throats. We were at each other's throats, Paul informed me, because I was damned uncooperative from the start.

In a fit of masochistic indulgence, I tortured myself for the next few hours by reliving my entire encounter with Paul, again and again. *What a prick,* I thought. *Showing up after all this time, waving old issues in front of my face—like a red flag in front of a bull.*

And he got to me. In spite of my brave words to Carla about being tough and together, the bastard got to me. Had me screaming and snarling and on the defensive all over again. When I pointed out that *he'd* had the affair that tanked our marriage, he informed me he'd had an affair with one woman, and was now married to that woman. When I told him I had multiple lovers now, he said he was sorry to learn I'd degenerated into a promiscuous way of life, while he had moved forward into the New Age.

Fuck you, Paul! Fuck you! Promiscuous, am I? You bet your sweet thing I am. I've had more fun, more honest pleasure with a pack of perfect strangers than I ever had with you. What do you think of that, you son-of-a-bitch? And I'm not through yet—not by a mile.

Jake called that afternoon. I felt a sense of relief at the sound of his voice. My men were what I needed.

"So how was the visit with your old man last night? Was it rough?"

"Was it rough? Do you have a few spare hours? I'll tell you how rough it was." I sank down on the sofa feeling sorry for myself.

"Did you have sex with him?" Jake asked, getting right down to what he clearly considered the nitty gritty of the situation.

"No, I didn't have sex with him. Why would you even think that? I loathe the son of a bitch!" I heard my voice rising. The phone was clenched in my hand

Jake laughed. "I just thought you might have, sweetheart. You're still hung up on the guy, aren't you?'

"The hell I am! What makes you think that?"

"I think that because I hear how upset you are. And the reason you're so upset is because your old man don't see you the way you want him to see you. And as long as you still care what he thinks, you're still hung up on him."

There was an unpleasant ring of truth to those words that enraged me all the more. I rose from the couch and walked around the room, dragging the long twisted phone cord along with me.

"Damn it, Jake, have you thought of studying psychiatry? Well, I guess in your own way you have. But for your information, I don't give a damn what Paul thinks of me! In fact, after last night, I'm so grateful he's married to Cassandra instead of me, I'm thinking of sending him a thank-you note!"

Jake wasn't into arguments and didn't pursue the subject. Instead, he said, "Listen, Dorothy, do you want me to come by tonight?"

Did I want him to come by tonight? Did I want to take a journey into fantasy is what he meant. Did I want to go out into the night, to play and be wild—to ease my inner aching with the magic of the moment? Even as I considered it, I felt my body flush and my mood changed abruptly.

"Yes," I said, and my voice grew husky in response to my excitement. "Why don't you come by about ten, after the kids are in bed and kidnap me?"

There was a brief silence while Jake considered my request. I visualized his dark hooded eyes gleaming and his mouth curved up into a smile as he ran the scenario around in his mind. "You wanna be kidnapped, huh? OK, sweetheart, you got it. One kidnapping coming right up."

I sat very still in the front seat of Jake's truck as we drove along the Great Highway, gazing from my window into the darkness of Ocean Beach. "Let's get kinky," Jake said and bound my hands behind my back with a scarf. My legs were spread apart under my flowing tie-dyed skirt and I wore nothing beneath it. The foggy night air felt cool and delicious between my legs. I can't say why, but being bound that way was incredibly arousing. We drove in silence. Every now and then I stole a timid glance at the dark, hulking stranger who'd captured me, wondering who he was and where he was taking me—and what he planned to do to me when we reached our destination.

"Spread them legs, woman," Jake said, affectionately, while his knowing fingers slipped beneath my skirt. "Just wait till I get you home. I'm gonna make you submit to my basest desires."

A jolt of excitement shot between my legs like an electric shock. "Mmmm," I purred, closing my eyes; "doesn't sound half bad."

We drove in silence for a while. Then, I opened my eyes again and took a long, dispassionate look at Jake. It was a poignant moment for me.

"You're the perfect stranger," I said slowly. "Perfect—*because* you are a stranger."

Jake was amused. "Oh I'm pretty strange, all right," he said and laughed.

I smiled, recalling my girlhood dream of finding the one perfect man who would be everything to me— lover, partner, companion, friend—which turned out to be nothing more than a fantasy, after all.

"At least this way it doesn't hurt so much," I said under my breath.

"What'd you say, sweetheart?" Jake asked. "I didn't catch that."

"I said you're pretty strange, stranger, but that's fine with me. Say, what kind of abductor are you, anyway? Take me home this minute and hold me for ransom. And while you're holding me, well, I might just struggle and try to get away..."

I was back in the fantasy now and gave my lover a long, intense look. "I might even call for help... Like this: help, help," I whispered.

Jake and I were memorable that night. He blindfolded me and went down on me until I came. Then, with his rock-hard cock thrust up inside me and my fingers teasing my clit, I came again. Later, curled up with Jake and bathed in afterglow, I felt certain that Paul's ghost—with all its harsh judgments on my life— had been driven from my consciousness and consigned to wherever it now belonged.

Part Five—1977

How Many Notches Do I Make On My Gun, Before The Handle Falls Off?

Dear Carla,

After almost a month of procrastinating, I'm finally sitting down to write. Truth is I've been putting this letter off because I kept hoping that if I did, the problems I want to discuss with you would have miraculously worked themselves out. And I *so* wanted to write you another glowing report on the smashing success of my perfect single life. However, such are the fortunes of war that this is not the case. The issues that have troubled me for a while now are troubling me still. So brace yourself, Carla. Once again, I'm about to cry on your sturdy shoulder via the U.S. mail.

So what's the big problem, you ask? Good question. Precisely the one I'm attempting to pinpoint myself. Well, first of all, that little voice inside my head, the one that keeps whispering—*something's wrong with your life, Dorothy*—is back. Only now it's not whispering, it's shouting!

To make matters worse, it doesn't restrict itself like it used to, to times when I'm alone. Oh no, it makes itself heard at all sorts of inopportune moments. For instance, when I'm lying under some perfect stranger and all of a sudden I'm looking up at the guy, thinking, *who the hell are you?* Well, I don't know who he was. But the point *is* that didn't trouble me before...

What's going on with me, Carla? Nothing seems to turn me on anymore. Last week, for example, Arthur—my wealthy lover, flew me to LA for a luxury weekend at the home of some movie producer friends who were swingers. Clear offered to stay with the kids, leaving me free as the proverbial bird in the sky and off to enjoy the good life with all expenses paid.

Sounds great, right? So sophisticated and free, right? Well, wrong. The whole time I was in that luxurious LA mansion with its nine bedrooms, kidney-shaped swimming pool, and full staff of servants, my intention was to stay in the fantasy and have fun.

Somehow though, I found myself outside of it, a lonely observer studying the other players in the game. There was the producer's wife, twenty years my senior, size three and newly face-lifted. The young starlet, a Clairol blond, with big breasts and bigger ambitions. Her lover, a real estate broker with sweaty hands. And there was the producer himself, whom I found to be a cold and shallow man, not to mention an insensitive lover.

So, when even a mini-orgy and a perfect orgasm don't thrill me like they used to, I know something's wrong. I'm feeling oddly like I did when I was married—dissatisfied, bored, and lonely even when I'm not alone. *I want something more!* the voice in my head keeps shouting. Hell, I'd be more than happy to give it any damn thing it wants, if I could just figure out what that thing is.

Oh Carla, sometimes I feel so confused. I mean, do I want perfect strangers who keep me emotionally safe but leave me lonely? Or do I, could I, deep down inside want someone like Stuart whom I've kept at arm's length since the night I first realized he cared for me?

Why, you ask? Because he scares the hell out of me, that's why. Hey, he's the sort of man who asks a woman to marry him and makes commitments, and might even want to cherish me until death did us part—which as we know, doesn't work out for most of us and when it ends, the hurt goes on and on.

I don't know how to deal with heavy stuff like that.

As though all of this isn't enough, lately I've been feeling an urge to stop drifting along in life and do more with these talented hands than stroke an endless series of cocks...

Last month I made a new friend, Toni, a woman artist who supports herself by making pottery and selling it at craft fairs and wholesaling it to small artsy shops. I visited her studio last week and spent the whole afternoon throwing pots on her wheel and building a few clay creatures. I was pretty rusty, but that was the first time in three years I've felt clay in my hands. I can hardly describe how good it felt.

You know, Carla? I still have that few thousand dollars from the sale of my house squirreled away. And it occurs to me that if I offer to pay her, Toni might let me work in her studio on a regular basis so I could build up an inventory of pieces to sell. It seems possible that if I did this, I could be on the way to the career as an artist I've always wanted. Exciting thought, don't you think? Stay tuned. I'll let you know what happens next.

In the meantime though, the rest of my life remains in turmoil. If you have any stray thoughts on how I might best deal with seven steady boyfriends and a platonic friend named Stuart—please put them in an envelope and mail them, special delivery, to the usual address.

Love,
Dorothy

P.S.—The kids are doing fine and growing at an alarming rate. Brad had a part in his school play. He was terrified of forgetting his lines, but didn't—and although of course I'm completely biased, I thought his acting was really good. Doug required four stitches soon after joining the school hockey team. I can't wait until the season gets further underway.

CHAPTER THIRTEEN

Even when I knew in my gut that a big change was coming—coward that I was, I resisted it for as long as I could. Looking back on it, I'd say it was more than a bit frightening to feel the newly laid structure of my brave new life begin to crumble around my shoes.

With renewed enthusiasm born of desperation, I threw myself into my swinging single life. Making some last-ditch effort to recapture the satisfaction I'd found in it just a year before. The fantasies flowed fast and free as I stepped up the pace and played myself into a state of near exhaustion—in the interest of preserving what I persisted in calling an uncomplicated life.

With an impressive burst of energy, during the three weeks that followed, I dined and danced with Arthur. Swayed to the music at a rock concert with Curt. Took in an astrology lecture with Steve. Had a winning afternoon at the race track with Jerry. Attended the opening of a light show with Joel and, finally, sat through an intellectual foreign film with Richard.

As if all of this wasn't entertaining enough, there was sex for entertainment too. There was sex on a shag rug. Sex in a rental car at the race track parking lot after winning $1,000. Sex on Ocean Beach with an orgasm in the moonlight and sand in my vagina—and, last but not necessarily least, sex on a plain ordinary bed.

I was having so much fun I could hardly stand it. I felt like I was moving faster than a speeding bullet— faster than light, even. But still, I was forced to admit that I couldn't outrun my changes. Like it or not, some new awareness had been born in me, and I found myself reflecting wistfully on how little closeness was shared between me and the perfect strangers with whom I was physically intimate with.

But that's what you wanted, Dorothy, I reminded myself. *You wanted, above all else, to keep it light and entertaining and hot and exciting. You wanted to know you would never again be trapped by your own overwhelming emotions, or controlled by your need to cling, or by having anyone cling to you. You wanted to enjoy any and all of them, without being in love with any one of them.*

And to know you could walk away at a moment's notice and feel no regret...

Yes, yes, that's true. That's what I wanted, and that's what I got. So why do I feel like crying most of the time?

I was still on the verge of tears when Jake arrived the next evening and took me in his arms. I pressed in close to his big warm body as though it might hold some comfort for me.

"You look down, Dorothy," he said, surprised and scrutinized me with eagle eyes to determine why. "I haven't seen you in over a week. Have you been getting laid enough?"

His concerned tone of voice was the same one my mother used when she called to ask if I was taking my vitamins and eating enough fruits and vegetables. In spite of my dark mood, I had to laugh when he said that.

"Yes, sweetheart," I said, "I've probably been laid enough to satisfy a small sex-starved country."

"So what's the problem?" he inquired—like what other problems could there be? His tone was almost tender though and for a crazy minute I considered telling him what was going on inside me and wondered, if I did, would he understand?

"Well," I began, "I've been feeling pretty down lately, and the reason is…" I stopped abruptly because Jake's attention had wandered and he was staring out the side window with interest.

"Wow!" he said craning his neck for a better view. "There's a couple making out on the couch in the flat across the way. Hey, she's a hot woman. Look at them hips move."

Momentarily distracted from revealing my inner feelings, I watched, not the woman, but Jake, in fascination. *Amazing*, I thought, *everywhere this guy goes, all he has to do is look out any window, and bingo!— someone nearby is having sex, or masturbating, or at the very least stark naked. The question is, does he somehow create them? Or were they there all along, just waiting for some natural born voyeur like Jake to catch them in the act?*

I was pondering this interesting question when Brad wandered into the room. "Hey guys, what's happening?" he asked.

"A couple's making out in the apartment across the way," Jake spoke in a hushed whisper, without shifting his gaze.

"That's great, Jake," I said, giving him a dirty look. "The kid needed to know that."

"Wow!" Brad said and rushed to look.

"What's going on?" Doug asked, entering the room.

"Oh boy," I said.

"A couple's making out in the apartment across the way," Brad told him, succinctly, without taking his eyes from the window.

"I'll go get the binoculars," said the kid, and ran from the room.

"Hold on," I said, stepping up to the window to lower the blinds. "Whatever those people may be doing in the privacy of their own home is their business entirely, and it's very rude of us to be watching them."

"No worries Dorothy," Jake said, grinning broadly, "They just rolled out of sight."

The strange little scene lightened my mood, on the outside at least. Later, after dinner when the kids were in bed, the conversation turned to sex again and I didn't get back to telling Jake what was troubling me. Like Scarlett O'Hara, I planned to think about that heavy stuff tomorrow—not tonight when my number one lover was here with me, and the moon was full.

As usual, he knew what I needed, or so he said. I admit, I had my doubts when his suggestion for the evening was a swing party at a private house across the bay. But Jake, with dogged persistence, overrode my objections one by one, selling me on the place like he owned stock in the company.

"There's a full moon tonight, in Scorpio. What you need tonight, Dorothy is something hot and explosive," he said with authority, and finally I agreed with him, hoping that at least one of us knew what I needed.

Perfect Strangers

Perfect Stranger Encounter #11

Jake And A Green-Eyed Stranger

My mood lightened somewhat during the twenty-minute ride across the bay. I was out into the nighttime once again, leading with my sexuality and dedicated to the concept of never being lonely or sad. Still, some part of me was hesitant, wondering precisely how the desire for intimacy I'd been feeling lately could be satisfied by a group of people I didn't know.

The swing party was in full swing by the time we arrived. It was, in fact, eighty-six people strong.

"A very nice turnout," Herb, our host, informed us with modest pride. "We get a lot of comebacks you know."

I stood in the entryway looking around. From there I could see most of the main floor—the living room, dance floor, kitchen, and sun porch beyond. Two things I noticed right away—almost everyone was towel-clad or naked, and almost every light bulb in the place was red. All around me, men and women were checking each other out. Sex vibrations zapped back and forth like balls on a tennis court.

I turned to Jake to see what he thought of all this. He was busy assessing the situation. His eyes roaming boldly, sizing people up. I watched him, feeling the intensity of his attention.

Christ, I thought, *he's almost sniffing the air.*

"OK, sweetheart," he said finally. "Let's lose the clothes and go look around."

We emerged, towel-wrapped from the dressing rooms. Hot eyes slid over my body reminding me I was desirable as I followed Jake down the hallway to begin the grand tour.

So what happens now? I wondered. Will Jake and Dorothy find bliss in the sperm-stained halls of Herb's house—or. any reasonable facsimile thereof? Stay tuned for the next exciting episode and find out.

Although I assured myself I was perfectly at ease, the truth is I wasn't and felt relieved when Jake suggested dinner before sex.

"Smoked oysters," I said, smiling as I helped myself to the buffet. "How appropriate."

As we ate, that vague, unhappy feeling in me began easing up and I relaxed into the party vibration. I observed the people around me. Curiously guessing at zodiac signs, speculating on possible sexual performance, and eavesdropping on conversations.

"Jill! It's so good to see you. It's been weeks!"

"Great roast beef, don't you think?"

"Have you been here before?"

"Try the quiche, it's delicious."

"So, what do you do for a living?"

"I come here often."

"We went to a party in Marin last weekend. Man, we had a ball! Ended up on the front lawn at six in the morning with these three…"

"I'm a Gemini. What sign are you?"

"How long have you been divorced?"

"Have you been here before? Or is this your first time?"

The grand tour continued after dinner.

"Now remember, Dorothy," said Jake, who was determined to get me in the mood. "An orgy is a growth experience."

"Oh, is it really?" I raised my eyebrows at that one and smiled in spite of myself.

"Oh yeah," he responded, sagely nodding his head. "You learn all about yourself when you strip away your clothes."

Interesting theory, I thought, checking out a passing cock. *Ohhhh, very nice…* And what better place to test such a theory—particularly once we'd left the main floor, which was used primarily for socializing.

Above and below stairs was another story.

The entire basement was a veritable rabbit warren of small curtained enclosures, designed for couples whose fantasy of the moment prompted them to hide away from the crowd—and in relative seclusion, have sex like, well, rabbits.

And it was roll your own in choice of creature comforts, or any particular atmosphere. There were mirrors, vibrators, water pillows, and silky mats. There was shades of the Arabian Nights, a red-curtained bed with black satin sheets and blood red pillows. There were, as well, enough jars of massage oil, cold cream, and tubes of KY Jelly lying around to grease a battleship, and a bowl of condoms as well. I had to admit that in the pleasure department, downstairs had possibilities.

Upstairs were four bedrooms, three of them small, and a huge master suite lined with mirrors and strewn with mattresses—which I knew without being told was the main orgy room.

"We'll stop back here later," Jake said, surveying the crowd. Several couples were necking and petting in various corners of the room. "They're all doing it two by two." His tone was disapproving. "I'll tell you, Dorothy, looks like there's some hot people here tonight, but looks to me they need someone to show them how to get down and orgy."

"Lucky for them you happen to be here," I said, straight-faced.

"Right on."

For Jake and me, the first action of the evening happened in the hot tub. There were four men and two women already soaking in it when we arrived. We climbed in and seated ourselves on the circular redwood bench. Everyone sat relaxing and watching each other—speculating, perhaps, on who might be doing what to whom, only minutes from now.

It was Jake, of course, who made the first move. Slowly and deliberately, his arms slid around my shoulders from behind and his big-boned hands cupped the fullness of my breasts. With a second smooth motion, he floated me up off the bench and set me down again on his waiting cock.

It is like shooting off a gun at a starting gate.

With a lustful look, the beefy guy with the overgrown chest hair across from us sat up on the edge of the tub and the full-bodied blonde beside him turned and went down on him. At almost the same moment, two of the men turned to the tall, stick-thin woman on my right. She looked them over, made her choice and climbed aboard the more attractive of the two.

Within three minutes of Jake's initial move, three of the men were screwing all three of the women—with the two left-over men looking lonely and waiting their turn.

The blond was bent over sucking hard. Just above the water line was her sizeable white ass. *Hey, we have a vacancy over here folks*, I thought and laughed aloud when the two extra men *raced* across the pool to get to her. The winner grabbed a condom from where he'd stashed it at the edge of the pool, rolled it on, slid into the blond, and began making waves.

The odd man out looked around hopefully. He eyed me with an ingratiating smile, but I looked away. A few minutes later he worked something out with the tall woman and friend.

After a while, the beefy man gave a groan as the blond sucked him off—while the little guy behind her created a small tidal wave as he shot his wad. He looked proud of himself at first, then lost and alone, as the original couple melted into each other, forgetting he was alive. He stood unsurely for a minute before climbing out of the pool, removing his condom, tossing it in the trash, climbing back in the pool, and sitting back down again.

"Shall we move on?" Jake asked when the little episode sloshed to a close. I nodded yes, and let him lead me from the hot tub room, wondering in a very unswingerly way, why, rather than exciting me to a fever pitch—the party was getting me down.

It was almost midnight when we arrived at the main orgy room because Jake insisted on making so many stops along the way. He reminded me of a man at a smorgasbord who was determined to get his money's worth. Since leaving the hot tub, we'd thus far played around on mats, pillows, shag rugs, a waterbed, and black satin sheets. Now, I supposed, foreplay was over and we were ready for the main event of the evening.

The room was filled with people. Half the house must have been in that one enormous room. A number of couples had gone to the mattresses, while others lay around fondling each other and watching others perform.

Jake paused when we'd stepped into the room and stood sizing it all up, not missing one thing that was going on. "Far out," he said with approval. "They're starting to get the idea. And maybe, I'll just give them a few more. Come on, sweetheart," he said taking my hand. "Let's go fuck around." His eyes gleamed with intensity as he led me to the center of the room.

Jake manipulated everyone.

Somehow, without being told, the entire group seemed to sense that a pro was among them, and showed their respect by accepting his fantasy as their own. Within fifteen minutes of our arrival, there was a pileup—one that made any group encounter I'd seen thus far, small stuff.

There were writhing bodies everywhere. And more moans and gasps and squeals than you'd hear in hospital intensive care. Everywhere I looked people were fucking and sucking and kissing and caressing. Everyone was somehow connected, like we were some kind of giant daisy chain. And since Jake had signaled the onset of the whole business by going down on me— I ended up on the bottom of the pile.

It wouldn't have been at all difficult to let go and get into it. In fact, I almost did. Hell, there I was being stroked and licked and sucked and nibbled, by everyone and his brother. I have to admit, a whole lot of it felt damned good.

What happened was, right in the middle of the orgy, that vague feeling of unrest and alienation came up again—and the little voice in my head started up, full blast. *Not now*, I snarled and grabbed onto the nearest cock in an effort to hush it up. *Can't you see I'm enjoying myself and don't wish to be disturbed?*

Leave me alone! I am having fun!

Are you sure about that, Dorothy? The voice wanted to know.

Sure enough, I thought, and raised my hips so a cock could slide in.

I lay there for a while attempting to lose myself in sensation, while the voice in my head went on and on, and snappy quick, just like that, the game I was playing stopped being fun. I looked around, bewildered. There were naked strangers all over the place.

"You're beautiful, love," someone said, and I shrank from the empty endearment. *Let me out of here*, I thought, as I pushed and clawed and scrambled my way to where I could see light again and get a breath of air.

"Whew!" I said when I was clear of the crowd.

"Taking a rest between innings?" a male voice behind me inquired.

I turned to the stranger who'd spoken. He was the lonely man from the hot tub. Up close, I saw he had a pleasant, sensitive face and rather large, beautiful green eyes that were oddly familiar—although I couldn't place where I'd seen eyes like those before. I regarded him curiously for a minute before turning my attention back to the mass of writhing people.

The orgy was going strong. Arms and legs and private parts were waving wildly in the reddish light of the room. Jake was all over the place, completely in his element—coaching and instructing and directing. Showing them all how it was done. Across the room, in the doorway, I saw Herb, our host, a happy man. Watching with a look of reverence on his face, at what may have been his number one orgy of the year.

"It's like...I'm watching that famous old film from the 1940s, *The Snake Pit*," I told the stranger. "You know, the one about a woman who cracks up, gets put into an insane asylum and ends up getting scared sane."

"And you, I presume, are Olivia de Haviland regaining her sanity," he responded with dry humor."

I thought that one over a minute before saying well, yes, perhaps I was.

We were silent for a while as we stared at the ongoing show.

"That guy's something else," the man said, indicating Jake. "He's really into it."

"Yes," I chuckled, as Jake rammed himself, with abandon, into a waiting body. "The man's a hedonist—driven by desire."

"I saw you come in with him. Is he your old man?"

I considered the question, imagining Jake in the

role of my old man. I thought about his good-natured lust for life's sensual pleasures. His incomparable ability to maintain a hard-on at any given moment in time. His unbending intention to please and satisfy all the sexually frustrated women of the world—not to mention his life, which had turned into one unending, sexual fantasy.

Wouldn't be half bad, I thought with a grin. *In a world without dependent children and as long as we never had to get out of bed.*

"I don't have an old man," I told the stranger, "I'm alone."

"Me too," he said observing the orgy with interest. "You know, I've been swinging since my divorce, four years now and let me tell you, this is one of the best parties I've attended so far."

"You really like it?" I asked curiously, and realized, with icy insight that I didn't. Not anymore. "I mean...not this one party. But you know...the whole scene."

He knew what I meant all right, I could tell. He knew all about nights spent laughing with perfect strangers because home meant being alone.

"Look," he said, "I play, I swing, I have fun. I enjoy it for what it is." He shrugged and smiled thinly. "And I don't get hurt that way... Do you know what I mean?"

"I know exactly what you mean," I said in a low voice. "We've been playing the same game."

We gazed at each other for a long drawn out moment, with big green eyes that were exactly alike. It was like looking at myself.

"Are you a Virgo, too?" I asked, finally. "And are you lonely?"

"Yes, to both questions." The man's face registered surprise. "How did you know?"

"I could see it in your eyes," I said and blinked back tears from mine.

For a minute we were very close to each other, like people are when they share an enlightening experience. The orgy sounds were building to a crescendo. Steve, that was the swinger's name, hesitated, as though unsure what he wanted to do next. Then, turning toward the action, he stood up and extended his hand. "Will you join me?"

I considered it—out of habit if nothing else. I looked him over. Not bad. Nice thighs. Nice buns. Nice thick cock. In fact, the man had all the makings of a perfect stranger...

I shook my head and smiled. "No. Thanks. I think I'm going to sit this one out. But please, feel free to carry on without me."

I hung out in the hot tub for a while and discouraged all offers of company. I was wrinkled when the orgy finally ran out of steam and Jake came to find me.

"Great party, don't you think?" he said as we climbed into his truck. "We really showed those folks how to get down and orgy." He was smiling. His voice was thick with triumph. Yet another fantasy had been orchestrated, courtesy of Jake. If he died tomorrow, he would not have lived in vain.

I was great too. We were both great. He pulled me close, draping his arm around my shoulders in a gesture of affection. "You and me, sweetheart," he said gazing down into my eyes. "We belong together. We're two of a kind."

I stared at him when he said that, curious for the first time in our relationship to know who he was. He wasn't about to tell me though, I could see the wall behind his eyes. He was and would remain by choice, a perfect stranger—mine to have and to hold, for as long as we laughed, and played and touched each other's fantasies—but never our hearts.

Two of a kind, are we? No, sweetheart, we're not, I thought, realizing that it was true. *My choice will be different after all.*

I was silent all the way home thinking about a lonely swinger with huge hurt eyes, while pondering the insights to be gained at an orgy of eighty-six people. *Jake was right after all*, I thought, grinning—*you learn all about yourself once you strip away your clothes.*

CHAPTER FOURTEEN

I didn't sleep well the night after the orgy. I kept having a terrible dream that all the men I'd ever made it with had assembled in my bedroom and were seated on wooden folding chairs, facing my bed like an audience. What made the strange scene even stranger was that Jake, my number one playmate, was the only man I was able to identify.

The others had no faces, only zodiac signs stamped across the front of their heads, and rulers where their cocks should have been.

"Why don't you have faces?" I called out to them, and they answered in solemn unison: "Because you didn't want to see who we were."

"Is that true? Is that true?" I called out again.

"Of course it's true, Dorothy, you unreasonable bitch!" a familiar voice snarled, and I turned to see Paul standing beside my bed.

"Who the hell invited you?" I asked, angered at the sight of him.

"You invited me," he said, coldly. "You take me with you wherever you go."

"No! I don't! It's not true!" I cried, and turned from him to Stuart, who'd somehow materialized at the other side of my bed.

247

"Make him go away," I begged. "I don't want him hanging around anymore."

"I can't do that for you, Dorothy," Stuart said. The corners of his blue eyes crinkled up when he smiled and he looked so kind. You're the only one who can do that—and you will, when you realize you don't need his approval to be who you are."

That wasn't the answer I wanted and I turned to Jake in the wild hope that maybe *he* was the one who could help me, and make Paul finally and forever, go away.

"I can't do it for you either, sweetheart," he said. "And I sure as shit tried, the only way I knew how."

"We all tried," echoed the crowd of faceless men, like some bizarre Greek chorus. "And we tried, and we tried, and we tried, and we tried…"

As I stared at them, the scene shifted and my men and I moved together through time and space in a way that made no sense at all. *ZAP!* My bedroom was gone and Paul and I were standing in our former home near Syracuse New York.

"No room! No room!" he kept shouting, like the Mad Hatter in *Alice in Wonderland*. I opened my mouth to shout back at him, and *ZAP!* The two of us were racing around Golden Gate Park playing a strange, surrealistic game—which as near as I could figure out, involved each of us embracing every bush, flower, and tree that stood in our path.

"I'm going to win this game," I said, confidently. "I'm a hell of a player, you know."

I kept telling myself the whole thing was only a dream and I could wake up any time I wanted to. I couldn't seem to manage it though, and the dream continued on for what felt like a long time. Finally, the scene dissolved to the Yellow Brick Road that was the pathway to Oz—which looked for some reason, exactly like the Golden Gate Bridge.

"I suppose this is another growth experience," I remarked to Stuart, who stood at my side. He was wearing a business suit, which was odd because I'd never seen him wear one before. He flashed me a smile and reached for my hand, but it was Jake who answered.

"Of course it is, sweetheart. Just take a look around. There's no one else here but him who's wearing any clothes."

I looked around and froze as I saw he was right. I was completely naked and standing alone in the center of the circle of naked men.

"Let's have an orgy," one of them said. "Let's make Dorothy come."

"Let's make Dorothy come," the men chorused. "Let's make Dorothy come."

"Hold it, all of you," I told them. "That's a noble sentiment you've got there and tempting, I'll grant you that...but first, I've got to decide what *I* want to do with my life..."

The men fell silent and remained motionless, waiting for me to decide.

"I've got no idea," I whispered after a long silence. My lack of knowing depressed me. I felt the prickling of tears in my eyes and, bitterly, I began to cry. And as I stood there with tears running down my face, a dense fog rolled slowly and heavily in from the sea. It obscured everyone—even Jake, and Stuart, and Paul, from my view—until I was left standing alone on the Yellow Brick Golden Gate Bridge to decide my direction.

The last thing I remember before I woke up was hearing someone—the Wizard I believe, or was he really a Wizardess?—say with authority, "The secret of happiness, Dorothy, is right in your own backyard."

"But I don't have a backyard!" I wailed. "I live in an apartment building."

"So wing it, stupid," the voice said impatiently. "Do the best you can with what you've got."

Possibly, the only thing worse than having a weirdo dream like that one is to wake up in the morning and immediately remember the whole wretched thing. *Rise and shine, Dorothy*, I told myself. *A brand new day has dawned.*

"Yuck," I said aloud and staggered around like a zombie getting the kids fed and off to school. I breathed a sigh of relief when I finally shooed them out the door, lunches and homework in hand, and I was free to drag myself back to bed.

I'm tired, very tired, I thought and shuffled down the hallway towards my room.

Small wonder, said the little voice in my head. *The way you run around. Who do you think you are anyway, Superwoman?*

Oh go back to sleep, I thought, irritated. *Its early morning.*

It sure is. And you feel like a wreck because you were out until all hours attending an orgy and hardly got any sleep. And didn't you have a high old time?

"If I simply ignore you, you will have to go away," I said aloud. "And that is my plan."

You can't ignore me forever, Dorothy, the voice called out, but I refused to respond. With dignity, I stalked to my room and began climbing into bed. I stopped short when I happened to glance up and caught my own eyes in the big mirror across from my bed.

I saw a tired woman looking back at me—a swinging single, if you please, who'd gone out on four dates in the past week, and five the week before—and who'd fallen asleep from sheer exhaustion on three separate occasions, under four talented men. She was pale and drawn, with deep circles under her eyes. I stood staring at her for a long time.

"Are you fucking more and enjoying it less?" I asked aloud, with a mocking smile. "Do you secretly long for love and affection, while playing it cool, and keeping it casual? Does sex with men with no faces leave you feeling cold and alone? If so, why not try a different lifestyle? This one, dear, is obviously getting the best of you."

I took a deep breath, ran my hands through my

hair and exhaled, slowly. *More than a hundred lovers in less than four years,* I thought with a weary sigh. *And where will it end? How many will it take to convince you that you're beautiful and desirable, and dynamite in bed—and to prove without a doubt that Paul was wrong in his judgments of you?* Pausing, I traced the circle beneath one of my eyes. *Question is, Dorothy; how much proof do you need? And practically speaking, how many notches can you make on the gun, before the handle falls off?*

There was a long silence.

You're scared, aren't you, dear? I asked myself. *You don't want to be a wife, you're bored with casual relationships, and you're just plain scared to be alone. You thought you'd found your niche as a sexual game-player who never let anyone in close enough to hurt you—but now you've come to realize you're not the cold-blooded swinger you thought you were. And that freaks you out, doesn't it? Because you've got no idea what other choices there are.*

So, here's an even bigger question: is there a life after promiscuity? Do you want to know for sure?

My image said nothing at all. She stared back at me, her large green eyes brimming with tears until the silence began grating on my nerves, and the tears spilled over and began running down my face. *I need someone to talk to,* I told myself. *I need someone loving, and loyal, and truthful at all costs, to help me figure things out and to decide: Where do I go from here?*

I suddenly knew with certainty exactly who that

someone was.

Okay, I told the little voice in my head, *I'm ready to talk with you now.*

Perfect Strangers

Epilogue

The Other Side, Of The Other Side, Of The Rainbow

Dear Carla,

Isn't it amazing that just when you get your life under control, with everything neatly arranged, the way you think you want it, not long afterward, crash bang—the whole bloody thing falls apart?

Since my own life has recently followed this unfortunate general pattern, I took this interesting question to my friendly local guru, who told me this happens because there is no growth without change and no change without growth—and that this is the nature of life itself and a universal truth.

Now isn't *that* bit of wisdom a mouthful and a half? In fact, I've been kicking the whole thing around in my head for a while now, thinking that if this is indeed true—well, it's a real pisser as far as I'm concerned. I mean, who said I wanted to change or grow at all? Maybe I liked my life just as it was, and can't help wishing, a bit wistfully, that everything could have stayed the same.

255

However, it hasn't worked out that way. I sure hope I've grown, Carla, because around my house things have changed a lot! You haven't heard from me since before the night of the giant orgy that Jake and I attended almost two months ago, so let me fill you in on what's been going on here in the Land of Oz.

First of all, as I look back on it, that orgy was, for me, the climax of my swinging single life. That night, although I never had a vaginal orgasm or any other kind, I did have at least forty-seven major insights into my own motivations and behavior—which led me to take a long look in my mirror the morning after— which led me, kicking and screaming, to have a long honest talk with myself.

Once I did this, it didn't take me long to come to the following, shocking conclusions: 1) my exciting life as a player had actually begun to bore me to death; 2) what was missing from my life was love and affection; and 3) unfortunately, it takes more than casual intimacy with a pack of perfect strangers, to make a liberated woman.

So now I know the truth. Oh boy. No wonder it's said that ignorance is bliss.

And what happened next? I can hear you asking. What happened after all the major insights, revelations, and conclusions were in and I knew with inner certainty that strangers—exciting and perfect though they appeared to be—couldn't give me what I really wanted? And what became of Stuart? And what became of Jake? And what, for Christ's sake, happened when my fun game of my way or the highway got called on account of rain?

Well, Stuart finally (as my mom might have put it) came out and declared his feelings for me in his gentle, soft-spoken way. He took me to dinner at China Station, a place in the Castro, with cozy wooden booths and amazing black bean sauce. We munched egg rolls with hot mustard and sipped jasmine tea from small, flower-patterned porcelain cups. And he took my hand in his, gazed into my eyes and told me he cared for me.

"We could make a good life together, Dorothy," he said. "I'd do everything in my power to do right by you and the boys."

I was silent when he finished speaking, while a jumble of confused thoughts and worries leaped around in my head, bumping into each other. Am I in love with Stuart, and blocking my romantic feelings for him because I fear commitment—or do I simply love him as a dear and trusted friend and not in an erotic way? Well, damned if I know.

And what if, worst case scenario, we became lovers and the sex wasn't good? Stuart wasn't Jake, after all—he wouldn't be sharing me with any stable of studs or anyone else for that matter. It would be just him and me in the relationship. And if it didn't work out between us—like it didn't with Paul—well, there'd be my kids getting hurt again, and I'd get ripped up too.

Stuart, sitting patiently across from me waiting for my response, looked so big and solid and stable and kind, I wanted to run to him for comfort—but I wasn't ready to trust my own feelings—and my newly emerged, tenuous sense of self was still way too fragile to be shared.

And my friend, Stuart, the best man I knew, deserved a lot more than that.

So I sat there with my eyes hot and stinging with tears, envying him the sureness of his feelings and wishing I could respond with that same degree of sureness, "Yes, I feel that way too."

In the movies, Carla, this scene would have played out differently. Trust me; Ellen Burstyn *would not* have turned this guy down. But, as the saying goes, if it feels right, do it and if it feels wrong, don't—and in the end, I did what felt right to me.

I told Stuart I couldn't say yes to him—at least not for now, and maybe not ever. And he understood, Carla. I could see it in his eyes along with his disappointment. There wasn't a great deal more to say after that. We left the restaurant in silence, mounted his motorcycle and, after buckling my safety helmet carefully onto my head, he drove me home. After dropping me at my door, Stuart told me to tell the boys goodbye for him and that he'd be leaving soon to go biking through Arizona and New Mexico for a while to explore new places and take time to think.

"I'll send you postcards and phone once in a while. I plan to be back in San Francisco by early spring of next year." He gazed into my eyes for a minute like he was thinking of saying something more.

But instead his hands stroked my shoulders and he bent to gently kiss the top of my head.

"Beautiful Dorothy," he murmured, before climbing onto his motorcycle and driving away. "We'll always be friends."

Jake, although he never mentioned the word love, in his own unique way declared his feelings for me too. He said that since our sexual fantasies fit together so well, what if we were to live together in an open relationship, of course. I kissed him tenderly before turning him down—and telling him I didn't want to ruin the only perfect relationship I'd ever had by trying to make it into something it wasn't meant to be.

His eyes widened when I said that and I think he was disappointed. But being a man who rolls with the punches, he soon found himself a sexually frustrated, forty-one-year-old woman, with an elegant apartment in Pacific Heights. She'd recently divorced a diamond merchant after a lackluster, seventeen-year marriage and was willing to consider live-in liberation.

"I've got my work cut out for me," Jake says, with a broad gleam in his eyes. "This poor woman has never experienced an orgasm of any kind in her entire life!"

In case you're wondering how I feel about Jake's having a new first lady of liberation to focus his attention on, the answer is just fine—especially since he comes by every week or so to make sure I'm not being sexually deprived.

Now, that's really thoughtful. I love a man with a strong sense of responsibility.

And what about my stable of studs, you ask? Well, it dissolved quite naturally, with no conscious effort on my part, once I became less available—having shifted my energy from having sex with strangers to creating forms out of clay.

Yes, Carla, that's my big news for tonight. Two months after ringing in 1978 at home with my sons—I began sharing my friend Toni's ceramic workshop and since then I've been working there every minute I can spare from the kids and my job.

And Carla, my pottery is taking off! I've sold some bowls and platters and two of my little clay creatures to friends and folks in the neighborhood, almost without trying and if I say so myself, I'm producing some decent work. Toni estimates that by spring I'll have enough pieces to do my first craft fair and to begin making my living doing what I've always loved to do. When this happens, I'm planning to quit my job here at the coffee house and work with clay full time.

We'll be moving too. Clear and I are leasing a flat together in Bernal Heights. A currently obscure but up-and-coming neighborhood. It's a beautiful place—a big old Victorian with bedrooms galore and an extra room off the kitchen. The kids, my boys and her girl, will each have a bedroom. Clear and I will each have one too and may rent out the extra one to cut down our expenses.

Hey, if you get fed up with Ray, or the kids, or icy Syracuse winters, why not wear a flower in your hair and come to San Francisco to hang out with us. Now, wouldn't that be a trip. The three of us women together? Clear's a confirmed player, you're the until-death-do-us-part, marrying kind, and me? I still don't know for sure. Maybe one day I'll meet a man with Stuart's steadfastness and Jake's brand of fine madness, all rolled into one hot, horny, potential life partner, and stepdad for the kids—and then maybe then I'll take a chance on love again. In the meantime, I'm checking out the other side of the *other* side, of the rainbow.

I guess that's all I have to say for now. Just wanted to reassure you that in spite of all the whining and worrying I've gone through about what's going to happen and what do I do when it does, things appear to be working themselves out once again. Ha, ha. You told me so. I'm a swimmer after all.

Still, in light of my recent experiences I would like to go on record as saying: if I was a salmon and had a choice, for sure, I'd choose to swim downstream instead of up because frankly, it would be so much less work. However, since arguing with the natural order of the universe appears to be a big waste of time, it's upstream I go—laughing and crying, changing and growing—taking myself to where I want to go. It's not half bad.

In fact, life is looking fine.

Love,
Dorothy

About Dorothy Freed

At 73, Dorothy Freed claims to be the oldest, practicing erotica writer in the SF Bay Area. This may or may not be true, but it's her story and she's sticking to it. Dorothy Freed is the pseudonym of a Bay Area writer, who lives with her husband, two senior rescue dogs, and a formerly, feral grand-cat in a coast-side community near San Francisco. She combines the roles of being a humane human, who stands up for animals and the natural world—with being a writer of sizzling hot, erotica. Her stories are memoir-based, inspired by her participation in the casual sex lifestyle, and later, the BDSM Scene.

Dorothy's website, (dorothyfreedwrites.com) contains her blog, *Sixty-Nine And Still Sexual.*

More Stories By Dorothy Freed

Plug Play
Featured in, ***The Big Book Of Submission Volume 2***
Edited by Rachel Kramer Bussel

Gold Standard
Featured in, **Tonight, She's Yours: Cuckold Fantasies II**
Edited by Rose Caraway

I Really Do Belong To You
Featured in, **The Sexy Librarian's Dirty 30, Vol. 2**
Edited by Rose Caraway

Full Body Massage
Featured in, **Dirty Old Women: Erotica by Women of Experience**
Edited by Lynx Canon

Love Sling
Featured in, **FOR THE MEN: And The Women Who Love Them**
Edited by Rose Caraway

Two Doms for Dinner
Featured in, **Best Women's Erotica of the year Vol. 1**
Edited by Rachel Kramer Bussel

The Corset
Featured in, **Dirty Dates: Erotic Fantasies for Couples**
Edited by Rachel Kramer Bussel

The Gambler
Featured in, **Sex Still Spoken Here: An Erotic Reading Circle Anthology**
Edited by Carol Queen, Jen Cross, and Amy Butcher

A Timely Correction
Featured in, **Cheeky Spanking Stories**
Edited by Rachel Kramer Bussel

Seduction Dance
Featured in, **Twice the Pleasure: Bisexual Women's Erotica**
Edited by Rachel Kramer Bussel

After Twenty-Eight Years
Featured in, **Ageless Erotica**
Edited by Joan Price

Adventure at the Casa Cervantes Hotel
Featured in, **The Mammoth Book of Quick & Dirty Erotica**
Edited by Maxim Jakubowski

Plaster Orgasm
Featured in, **Seattle Erotic Art Festival: Literary Art Anthology, 2012**
Edited by Kerry Cox